AF263621

Some Thoughts I've Picked Up Along the Way, II

Karen Barlow Parmiter, Ph.D.

ISBN: 978-1-4958-3105-8

Printed in the United States of America

Published September 2022

INFINITY PUBLISHING
1094 New DeHaven Street, Suite 100
West Conshohocken, PA 19428-2713
Toll-free (877) BUY BOOK
Local Phone (610) 941-9999
Fax (610) 941-9959
Info@buybooksontheweb.com
www.buybooksontheweb.com

To My Reader

The last time I had the opportunity to reference my world (my inner world) was through a book originally published in 2008, entitled, "Some Thoughts I've Picked Up Along the Way."

It's now 2022. At this point, life has awarded me advanced membership in senior citizenship – both through its organizations and the nature of the mail I'm receiving – mainly targeted toward ongoing, physical, maladies, plus future, residential and interment possibilities.

But hopefully, aging has granted me even more – added experience and added learning. And this being the case, "Some Thoughts I've Picked Up Along the Way, II" was born.

In both texts, my hope and intention remain the same: thoughts are offered that can present, review, revise, and/or formulate ideas, passions, or emotions on the part of the reader. Whatever our age, our thoughts, transported by our words, cannot be down-played. They define the best and the worst of our humanity.

DEDICATION

Obviously, no set of philosophies is universally embraced or adopted. It appears, however, that those which lead the individual toward finding a degree of inner happiness, love, hope, and peace are those which man looks to adopt.

This book contains some thoughts I've picked up through living. It's not meant to judge those of the reader. In the event, however, that they cause a second thought – on the part of the reader – then the text has been of value and served a purpose.

Virtually everyone has thoughts. We seem to be on the right page, however, when our thoughts, (translated into action), help to make our life better.

Some Thoughts I've Picked Up Along the Way, II

——— Speaking "Broken English" to a foreign speaker does not make you bilingual.

——— Many of the "things we're saving," if saved too long, do no one any good.

——— Our "inner world" is our "real world." (It's the one that knows us vs. the one the world knows).

——— No one has, or knows, all the answers.

——— One of mankind's greatest anxieties is loneliness.

——— God's Justice is not a surprise; it's His timing which often is.

——— True blessings find little room in an unforgiving heart.

——— True blessings find little room in a heart filled with resentment.

—— Time may be better spent in correcting our self-image, than in protecting it.

—— I once saw a sign that read: "I pray. God pays."

—— Adversity becomes a good thing when it results in our becoming stronger.

—— It's actually very scary how easily people can be manipulated.

—— If you can't think for yourself, someone else is bound to do it for you.

—— Some resent even constructive criticism.

—— If the present can be viewed as a positive step toward a better future, we've been rewarded wisdom.

—— Our words and actions become our children's strengths or weaknesses.

—— Only few live long enough to accomplish all one's desires.

—— Kindness should never be viewed as weakness, nor should meanness ever be viewed as strength.

—— Note: life is a school; however, its process is reversed. In school we get the lesson, and then the test. In life, we get the test…then the lesson.

—— Life often provides a re-test until we pass.

—— Time teaches. We each decide whether to take notes or not.

—— Want to laugh? Wait about 10 years. Then, look at the hairstyles and clothes you once proudly sported.

—— If you've tried to live someone else's life, the price is a forfeit of your own.

—— If given the chance, many would welcome an attempt to do some things differently.

—— When caught in a lie, self-preservation often motivates one's "first response."

—— How tightly we sometimes hold the purse-strings of our stinginess.

—— Few people look forward to dying, yet so many fail to make the very most of living.

—— Life repeatedly proves that kindness is a strength and meanness, a weakness.

—— Justice for the cowardly comes in many forms.

—— We often have multiple chances to learn from those whose ideas and ways differ from our own.

—— Even from the unappreciative, our kindness is never really wasted.

—— "Freedom" has many translations.

—— How quickly and how easily, we often justify our transgressions.

—— Injustice can more easily be forgiven, when void of the ingredient: "intentional!"

—— Want a personal lesson? Look back (after passing years) at some of your Facebook photos and/or comments.

—— Heroism: true love in action.

—— No one acts smart all the time.

—— Without Faith and Trust in a Higher Power, life easily becomes a meaningless struggle.

—— Don't you sometimes wish that you could fool yourself, as easily as you can fool the world?

—— At times, our greatest fault lies in what is not spoken, than in what is.

—— Many titles are worthy of praise…."Bully" is not among them.

—— Execution: the value or gift of every noble promise.

—— Many people are quite clueless about our country's past….as well as its present.

—— Our degree of happiness increases, when it's directed toward others.

—— Sometimes, our own stupidity surprises even us.

—— It's almost scary, how much our memory retains. ("Where did that come from"? we ask).

—— Our lives can lose some serious time, if insisting on knowing the "reason for everything."

—— Many hold the belief that someday we'll come to know the "reason for everything."

—— Somewhere between the dramatically daring and the habitually safe, live the general masses.

—— The negative mind views expectation as only an avenue toward disappointment.

—— "Skepticism" is sometimes warranted, but not as the guiding blueprint for one's life.

—— Academic settings are just one venue for opportunities of learning.

—— Man could often appear so much smarter, if just admitting: "I have no clue."

—— When "diversity" can only be seen as a problem, the longevity of the problem is almost guaranteed.

—— Our conscience has power….even affecting our physical health.

—— Recipe for holding on to our past hurts: think about them frequently. Talk about them constantly.

—— No matter how much evidence you think you have, you probably can't prove that yours is the dumbest sibling in the world!

—— "We'll see" is the classic come-back of the one who hopes never "to have to see."

—— If you want to become a victim of self-imposed fear, project all your possible future injuries due to the devices you now use.

—— One of our greatest gifts is to be truly loved.

—— A good educator never retires.

—— When our world opens beyond ourselves, then, we begin to fulfill our purpose.

—— "Force," is a strategy, which soon discovers it's limits.

—— Few strive to appear perpetually confused. It may just come naturally.

—— To be subjective is to be deceived.

—— If you never want to grow to be a better person, keep insisting you're perfect the way you are.

—— Flash: the world may not see you as your doting mother does.

—— Want to begin to think you really "have it all together"? Watch the Maury Povich Show.

—— Want to begin to believe you "have every neurosis/ psychosis known to man"? Watch the Dr. Phil Show.

—— "Pretending", may help create your world when you're young. It may create little, as you age.

—— Rest and relaxation are the demands of both our mind and our body….and they'll get their way.

—— Life sometimes mimics the game of hide-and-seek.

—— Trusting: the answer to life's problems. The Problem: in finding the who and what to trust.

—— To cope: one of life's ongoing demands.

—— It has been said that prayer is an attempt to bring things into focus, as they really are….as God sees them.

—— Man's brief prayer, in the worst of times, may simply be: "please help me."

—— We have many ways to express ourselves, yet there are times, when, all of them seem inadequate.

—— We grow in the silence, not in the clamor.

—— The older you get, the more easily you realize that all things are interdependent.

—— We eventually learn that we can often gain greater clarity through our heart, than through our eyes.

—— All that we've experienced has purpose.

—— Satisfaction is complete when our Soul is satisfied.

——— Periodically check — where your time and efforts are being spent.

——— Self- Abuse: to have never developed the ability to forgive.

——— Instant Frustration: trying to control every outcome of every situation in your life.

——— Instant Relief: after doing only what is yours to do, releasing your concerns to a Higher Power.

——— If realistically viewed: you're either living in harmony or in strife.

——— Only with time, do we begin to see how each phase of our life was necessary in our complex and miraculous transformation.

——— It's impossible not to realize the negative forces in life. It is possible, however, not to give them power over us.

——— The longer I live, the more evidence I find, in the affirmation: "all things work together for good."

——— Our choice: a focus on our Faith or on our fear.

——— No one moves forward before forgiving.

——— Unless relinquished, no one can take our attitude.

——— Man's body can be enslaved, but not his Soul.

——— Our degree of peace is easily detected by our thoughts, words, and actions.

——— Being generous is admirable; being generous to those who are unkind to us, is even more admirable.

——— I once read: "when I expand my mind, my heart often follows."

——— The real test of Christianity is to be able to bless those who have hurt you.

——— When "Ultimate Justice" is totally believed, no harm or injustice has power over us.

——— At times, the most difficult — (though important) — person to accept is oneself.

—— Our admission of weakness can lead to our greatest strength.

—— Change your attitude. Change your life.

—— A choice: to promote peace or stir up strife.

—— The idea is to have an open mind, not an empty one.

—— Formula for frustration: trying to change another person to your specifications.

—— Oftentimes, our freedoms become the avenues toward our confinement.

—— As we progress though life, our definition of prosperity almost always changes.

—— As we continue to live, our definition of beauty almost always changes.

—— The more we believe in Divine Order, the more we see it manifested in our lives.

—— Real change happens from within, then moves outward.

—— As a whole, man needs a sense of belonging.

—— In varying degrees, we all need to stay connected with one another.

—— Even the most serious of people need moments to become totally loose….It's called Balance.

—— "To act" is best reserved for the theatre.

—— Only God has the right to demand that title and its demands.

—— Beware how much you put off or postpone. Life sometimes doesn't allow a re-scheduling.

—— Quality is not always an in-born entity.

—— So often: man's vengeance never fully "evens the score." Never fully!

—— Hopefully, a person learns and practices one of life's biggest joys: giving back.

—— Sooner or later, all people must decide where to put their trust: man? Or God? Our life reveals our choice.

—— Who really decides a person's worth?

—— Who really decides a person's fate?

—— Worry, fear, anxiety, — do as much damage to our physical health, as a lack of exercise, smoking, drinking, etc.

—— Ironically, the only gift we hope to see returned, (and probably our most precious gift), is love.

—— Most people quickly begin to listen as the newest publicized warning begins: "bad drug," and then pray it's not been one of choice.

—— Many do compile a "bucket list." Some have worked on it; others can't even find it.

—— Sometimes mere perseverance can triumph over innate intelligence.

—— Most people are not as confident, or "as well off" as they pretend to be.

—— Think carefully on what you hope to inherit.

—— Not all inheritances are windfalls or even welcomed.

—— Some could never see themselves frequenting "The Dollar Store."

—— You can find some good stuff in "The Dollar Store." (As one who patronized them).

—— Household animals: what trumps pedigree? Heart-felt, unconditional love.

—— Happiness is seldom found in those who practice criticism and fault-finding.

—— In time, (among one's priorities), one becomes less bothered by the layers of perpetual, accumulating dust.

—— Time alters our motivation: like re-doing the wallpaper (or paint), changing the rug, moving the furniture, etc.

—— Observe some of our children's coaches: some appear more irrational than the irate parents.

—— Grand-parents can appear, at times, even more protective than a child's parents.

—— Most often, grand-children find us more tolerant and patient, than we are (or were) with their parents.

—— One of the greatest "perks" of old age can be our grandchildren.

—— Generally speaking, the two easiest chances of becoming rich: (1) inheriting money; (and/or) (2) marrying money.

—— If you live by your feelings, be prepared for an emotional and turbulent go-round.

—— We each have a choice: — how will I respond to what happens in my life?

—— Life can be viewed as never-ending challenges or ever-present opportunities.

—— Instant Frustration: — habitually comparing ourselves to others.

—— Instant Reminder: things of the world are temporary, but things of the Spirit are Eternal.

—— Simply put, forgiveness is an act of love.

—— True, outward expressions of peace must begin with true, inner peace.

—— God always holds the good in every situation.

—— When we use our gifts to help others, we're always blessed in return.

—— Never forget the people and situations that have helped you grow.

—— Whatever happened to the "love and good cheer" during those "after-Christmas-Day sales?"

—— No one knows everything….some just think they do.

—— How many of your shopping "bargains" actually turned out to be worthy of the title?

—— Rushed, exhausted, and irritated are not recommended as a shopper's demeanor — yet, they often take that form.

—— Family reunions can become an eventual battle ground.

—— The test of Patience: family get-togethers. The test of Tact: family get-togethers. The test of Memory: family get-togethers. The test of Kindness: (you already figured it out!)

—— College graduates need to represent themselves honestly. i.e., The University of Budapest doesn't exist.

—— The newest technology can become an immediate blessing or a long-term curse.

—— Act: just come up with a gimmick! Result: you could find yourself rich!

—— Some have told the same lies for so long, that now, even they believe them.

—— Scars that eyes can never detect are often the hardest to heal.

—— By the time you've learned a lot, you often don't have a lot of time.

—— Some people have all the answers to everyone else's life, but have few for their own.

—— Rewards come in many forms.

—— "Unlucky" can become the scapegoat for "incompetence."

—— Too many citizens are vastly uninformed regarding the rules that govern them.

—— Intelligence often has little connection to common sense.

—— How much of human energy is misplaced!

—— Few, who are irrational, angry, or intolerant will admit it.

—— Some believe man is governed by two masters: pain and pleasure, which determine man's fate.

—— Laughter plays many roles. It has even been used in an attempt to cover blatant ignorance.

—— Freedom, Justice, Truth: lofty sentiments, yet requiring constant effort to maintain.

—— Very, very few jobs are stress-free.

—— Surprises come in all forms.

—— It's often easier to "make fun of" the things we're "not knowledgeable about."

—— Ironically, things we pursue often elude us; when deciding to ignore them, they often entreat us.

—— Ironically, "giving away" oftentimes paves the way in "receiving more."

—— We really can become our own, worst enemy.

—— Some secrets are not shared, even between the closest of humans.

—— Cooking can be widely viewed as an art.

—— Impulsive words and actions pave the way toward long-lasting sorrows.

—— "Taking charge" may not be the desire, but nevertheless, may sometimes be the necessity.

—— Those who can be bought....can just as easily...be sold.

—— Woe be it to those, whose worth is solely based on money.

—— How quickly man can destroy, what it has taken nature decades to create.

—— Power can quickly change hands!

—— Money buys a lot...but not everything...nor everyone.

—— There may well be some things that man is not meant to know.

—— "Success" and "Failure" have many definitions.

—— Some days, the best we can hope for is: "just holding on."

—— Hopefully, before too long, we realize that inward peace is one of our greatest gifts.

—— A "good" or a "successful" day has many, different interpretations.

—— Humor allows the seemingly insurmountable to become momentarily bearable.

—— Laughter, like yawning, is an imitative response.

—— People sometimes fail to see the value in perseverance and determination.

—— Our siblings can both encourage us, and humiliate us…almost simultaneously.

—— Some people just don't like to mingle.

—— Some people just mingle too much — one reason they'll never be part of an academic, graduating class.

—— The funniest people are often those who don't even have that intention.

—— An affirmation often heard: there's not a spot, where God is not."

—— You're "entitled" when you've done the right thing to get it.

—— Our faith can grow stronger when the world has failed us.

—— When we're easily offended, we're prime candidates for unhappiness.

—— Staying angry is just another option, if your goal is to limit and alienate your life.

—— There's such a peace, when we just do the right thing!

—— Feelings buried alive...never die.

—— Our true feelings will always surface in some form.

—— At times, we can abuse ourselves — even more than anyone else can.

—— By the time we "get it right," we've used up a lot of the time to do it.

—— To grow old is assured; to grow wise is not.

—— It's important to be a generous giver; it's just as important to be a willing receiver.

—— Actually, life does come with a road map. It's our side-trips that can get us lost.

—— The more exceptions we place on our love, the weaker it becomes.

—— "The world" keeps going on, even when "our world" seems to stop.

—— We don't always have "to feel like" doing something, to do it.

—— Yours becomes an "exasperated" life, when trying to change the world around you.

—— Being a grand-parent: having a wonderfully subjective view of parenting.

—— Added satisfaction: remembering the effort behind our accomplishments.

—— Sometimes, we just need a little push.

—— The fortunate: those who can learn…before losing.

—— "Too late" are words we dread hearing.

—— Pressure can be motivating….too much, and it can be debilitating.

—— Our bank accounts do not necessarily represent the true worth of our lives.

—— Personal Health Care: somewhere between constant paranoia and total absenteeism.

—— Our financial estimates seem to invariably fail to anticipate those "unforeseen extras."

——— Giving of one's effort is sometimes more important, than giving of one's money.

——— Some vacations merely place our problems in different surroundings.

——— While life can appear to be a cruel teacher, its important lessons have a worthy goal.

——— Virtually all humans, at least at some point, need support.

——— Always make your own shadow — never become a blend of someone else's.

——— Periodically, it may be good to be somewhat impractical — maybe, just good for the Soul!

——— It takes real courage to admit our most hidden weaknesses.

——— It may well be argued that making war is not having the maturity to make peace.

——— Know your gifts. Know which ones you're willing to give away.

—— If you're not sure that you can afford it, you probably can't.

—— Some of our life experiences will invariably bring tears to our eyes.

—— Some of our experiences will always cause us to smile, or even laugh.

—— Not all our plans are meant to materialize.

—— Whatever "extreme" you've chosen, you've probably entered the realm of the "unhealthy."

—— Don't you get tired of all those commercials?

—— "Required to volunteer" / What's wrong here?

—— Our memories can ("conveniently") go into: "I don't (can't) recall" mode.

—— Whatever happened to: "your word is your bond"?

—— Some have decided to make few, if any, decisions.

——— It's somewhat of a blessing that our moods are so transient.

——— Want to see miracles every day? Watch how people drive, and are still alive.

——— More and more people live lifestyles that are making them look like human dumplings.

——— If you want to grade your discriminating taste, review the parade of your past dates.

——— "Whom can we trust?" Becomes an ongoing quandary.

——— Life has a way to "blind-side," even the most careful.

——— "Time" is uncontrollable — never in our power to hurry, slow, or stop.

——— To believe the best can at times be quite challenging.

——— Beware of companions who require constant proof of nearly all your words and actions.

——— "Moving forward," after an emotional collision, may seem impossible, but always a necessity.

——— Our greatest heartaches need three important helps: patience, people, and the passing of time.

——— Our present reality need not be our ultimate future.

——— Mistakes can be the motivator toward progress.

——— Obstacles become the tests of our Faith.

——— Self-pity puts "healing on hold."

——— Guilt only serves a purpose, if eventually, it becomes an agent for healing.

——— We never want the epitaph of our lives to read: "a comedy of errors."

——— Hope, Faith, Trust — always necessities.

——— Too easily, time can seem to just slip away.

—— Excuses: usually of little help….and even less value.

—— A premise of perseverance should not be: "how long you've managed to stay dumb."

—— Confrontation — though not encouraged — is sometimes a necessity, and unavoidable.

—— A true test of maturity is when we can honestly admit our inadequacies.

—— We're either always learning or merely existing.

—— Boredom: an environment of stagnation.

—— If your life has no message, it has little meaning.

—— "Pity" is not a desired component of love.

—— Unfortunately, we can praise with our mouths, while our hearts may not agree.

—— When confronted, what's our initial response?

—— If honest, the "Golden Rule" is a "Major Rule."

—— There are times, when we just want to be alone.

—— "Forgetting" can be both an unintentional and an intentional act.

—— Under "things to do": being thankful is a basic, not an extra.

—— Basically, our greatest blessings come from acts we choose to do, rather than those we're forced to do.

—— The greater control we place on our love, the weaker it becomes.

—— Don't get into the habit of "over analyzing" everything.

—— Observe Nature: it has much to teach us.

—— Even one's enemies can be a motivating force.

—— Children can teach us important lessons — many which we have forgotten too soon and too quickly.

—— Men and women are meant to be complementary, not combatant, to each other.

—— Adolescence is no easy time to live through!

—— Marital problems: often, the unresolved, immaturity of adolescence.

—— Emotional maturity is not part of the package of a college diploma.

—— We can no longer afford the thought of isolationism — as individuals or as countries.

—— We have begun to mature, when we begin to listen.

—— Boredom is just one element of unhappiness.

—— Some use conversation only as a platform for one's complaints.

—— Discussion is worthy, when the goal is worthy.

—— Hope is always available….but only when individuals become "available."

—— Being content or complacent is the ideal.

—— Religion can be interpreted far differently than spiritualism.

—— To be defiant is neither helpful, nor profitable.

—— Beware of those whose only motive is for financial and personal gain.

—— Being right is often no assurance of having peace.

—— There's never a need of people, who are anxious to evaluate, scrutinize, judge…others.

—— Some find it quite easy to criticize, yet somewhat difficult to encourage and praise.

—— "Things" offer no ultimate or permanent ownership.

—— "Interpretation": an avenue for possible growth or sustained prejudice.

—— "Competition": an avenue for possible growth or continued frustration.

—— We more readily gravitate toward those who usually agree with us.

—— The unhappy, frequently look for others to promote their philosophy of gloom and doom.

—— Lack of emotion…continual complacency….are shallow forms of living.

—— Cynicism becomes a detour from happiness.

—— What stirs the Soul can ignite one's transformation.

—— Self-importance — often the precursor to self-destruction.

—— In time, most people begin to realize that the Golden Rule is not an option.

—— Keeping things in perspective is more than a suggestion — it's a "must."

—— Ask yourself: how far will I go, in order to be accepted?

—— Ask yourself: whose acceptance am I trying to gain?

—— Very, very often, it's the battle against loneliness that the elderly ultimately lose.

—— A son or daughter may leave their mother's home, but never her heart.

—— The distance between family members may have nothing to do with miles.

—— Life may not allow "undoing;" but it can sometimes allow "redoing."

—— Scary: doing something wrong for so long that we're now convinced that it's right.

—— Some people are never satisfied!

—— At times, our greatest form of comfort can be "someone just being there."

—— Even when right, we can waste so much of our lives, trying to prove it.

—— Hopefully, we come to realize that God always knows the truth, and needs no proof.

—— Our struggles are on two fronts: those within us, and those outside us.

—— Peace is a gift; however, its attainment sometimes takes a lifetime.

—— Real stupidity: continuing on a path that we know will probably bring us little good.

—— Too many adults remain stuck in an adolescent (even childish) emotional state.

—— A spoiled upbringing normally produces a spoiled adult.

—— Beware: the leader who proclaims that his/her way is the only way.

—— It's unbelievable (and alarming) how much of us, our children live out.

—— Boredom can be a sign of being spoiled.

—— "To run away from our circumstances" is to go nowhere.

—— "Calm" is not always synonymous with inactive.

—— There's not always a second chance.

—— "Reaching out" doesn't mean banding together with other malcontents.

—— There are more things that man actually knows — but doesn't want to admit.

—— Our history may take a different slant, if asking a Native American or African American.

—— Many individuals are much more prejudiced than they're ever willing to admit.

—— Life is about "dancing"…not "sitting."

—— "The music" of dance is "Faith."

—— Complacence can seem difficult to attain.

—— Cynicism is skepticism.

—— Stubbornness is a stalemate.

——— Finding our purpose can mean finding our peace.

——— A test of maturity: ultimately choosing what's right, over the clamor of one's emotions.

——— Whether toward our betterment or our demise, time continues unceasingly.

——— "Advertising" targets nearly everything: losing weight; growing hair; losing lair; concealing fat; gaining muscles; buying; selling; finding love;……

——— The more complicated, the more open to error.

——— Few people have a totally, unselfish agenda.

——— Too often, we find out that what we thought we wanted….we shouldn't have wanted.

——— Always have the right motive for giving.

——— Countries with stricter laws, very often, can boast of lower offenses.

——— "Accountability and fear" have a definite correlation.

—— "Facebook" can: enlarge our world, re-connect our world, promote our world, even destroy our world.

—— "Good" has come to have many meanings…but fewer proofs.

—— Many come to truly understand (and become forgiving of) their parents, as they, themselves, age.

—— It would appear that few people ever find a true balance in their lives.

—— A healthy life: do what is yours to do….and know when to let go.

—— "Rich" is most certainly, a debatable term.

—— Just "trying" is often a reward in itself.

—— "Force": one of our greatest tools, if desiring "rejection."

—— The "lazy" use their "feelings" as a barometer for their participation or effort.

—— Faith: one of its greatest tests is waiting.

—— Beware both people and organizations to which you've pledged undying allegiance.

—— Growing older can birth new ideas, compassion, and inner strength.

—— Growing older, (for others), can birth increased stubbornness, resentment, and distrust.

—— Most know, even during an act, when it's wrong.

—— Some argue, simply to take the opposite view.

—— Doing anything out of guilt is fruitless.

—— You have a much better chance of changing yourself than those who frustrate you.

—— Choosing kindness over criticism, forgiveness over bitterness, will always prove the better choice.

—— Some of the best connections we can ever make have nothing to do with technology.

—— We have a way of attracting the best and the worst to ourselves.

—— Greedy? Selfish? — too often rationalized.

—— Nothing worldly has permanence.

—— Some never seem to untangle their tightly, knotted worries.

—— Some never learn to accept…and find peace.

—— Needing only to be right or to be in control is the choice of two, worthless battles.

—— Visit the ocean: it's proof of nature's rhythm, its miraculous creatures, its soothing peace.

—— Visit the ocean: it's proof of man's clueless response to heat, water, and attire.

—— When life becomes mainly work, we always pay a price.

—— Faith: the strength that allows us to see our immature son, as a competent parent.

—— Faith: the strength that allows us to see our flighty daughter, as a stable citizen.

—— Most things can be improved upon, simply by using basic, common sense.

—— We don't have "to make" as many of our opportunities, as we think we do.

—— How much of T.V.'s "reality shows" mimic the reality of most people?

—— Frustrated and petty would not appear to be chosen goals….yet result as the fate of many people.

—— What a ludicrous waste of time and effort, to continue to complain about what, we know, we can't change.

—— Power taken from us is sad, so is our power, when unused.

—— Temptation: created by those around us, those in media, and thoughts within ourselves.

—— Unhealthy — almost everything driven to the extreme.

—— Immaturity: to relish in another's misfortune.

—— Maturity: to be able to feel good, even for those who may have hurt us.

—— Wealth can even open doors to greater vices and greater fears.

—— Some premonitions really do come to fruition.

—— It's virtually unbelievable how the truth, that often tries to hide, is miraculously revealed.

—— The expiration date of "truth"? None.

—— Those, who are unscrupulous, often target those whose hearts are bigger than their brains.

—— Unfortunately, there are more actors just walking around than those actually in this profession.

—— The most important shopping spree you want to make is the one dealing with your health.

—— No one can promise another...total safety.

—— We can touch others, when we touch their mind.... but ultimately, when we touch their heart.

— It's the real survivors, who write history.

— Some never discover their purpose.

— Truth is immortal, and always surfaces…at some time…in some way.

— To the disheartened, the eternal, sustaining truth prevails: "with God, all things are possible."

— Not all races are ours to run.

— Some of our greatest blessings come through unexpected channels.

— Real Wisdom and Peace: Trusting the "Who" that is in control; Living the "What" that is directed; and Accepting the "Why" that is unknown.

— Knowledge can arrive sooner than understanding.

— "Acceptance" — can be either the badge of the cowardly or the crown of the wise.

— With time, the intangible proves stronger and more resilient that the tangible.

—— Weakness comes in many forms…as does strength.

—— Not everything we lose is a loss.

—— Our greatest purpose is often found and faced, when we go outside ourselves.

—— The last, three phases of many lives involve: loneliness, illness, and passing. The last two may be inevitable, but the first one need not be.

—— The quality of companionship is determined by the nature of the companion.

—— Discovery: finding something that was always there.

—— "Money's Best" — like love's best — is in knowing when to hold on, and when to let go.

—— Holding on to money too long — can be too long, even to benefit the holder.

—— We learn that it doesn't always happen "to someone else."

—— "Business as usual" has unfortunately come to mean ongoing graft and corruption.

—— Some have given up on the idea of being debt-free.

—— Never say never!

—— Material investments never include a 100% guarantee.

—— Very few days evolve problem and stress-free.

—— Some forms of beauty do last.

—— We never have the power "to see the whole picture."

—— Do we really want to be forgiven: "….as we forgive those who trespass against us"?

—— The seasons of most lives mimic the seasons of nature.

—— Though sounding contradictory, there are people who can be described as "humble leaders."

——— We all need rest…at some point.

——— At times, we make life more elaborate and costly than it has to be.

——— Our answers may not be what we expect or desire.

——— What we accept becomes just as important as what we reject.

——— Hurrying, itself, can actually become a waste of time.

——— All life-forms have something to teach.

——— It's only when we learn to slow down, that we can appreciate what we have.

——— Never forget the good within you — it always exists.

——— Many believe that nothing happens to us by chance.

——— We may need forgiveness for our unforgiveness.

—— Avoid: spending your present time in anticipating future struggles.

—— No physical object that we have is permanently ours.

—— It's not easy to always be honest and kind — but it's always worth the effort.

—— Eventually, the sun does come out.

—— With time, we're able to see the blessings, behind the storms in our lives.

—— There are times when the best steps we can take are "out of the way."

—— The less burdens we bear, the freer we are.

—— "Humility" can actually be taught…if willing.

—— Another's good fortune need not automatically be seen as our misfortune.

—— When we "give back," we demonstrate the understanding of what we've been given.

—— Wisdom: knowing whose voice you will hear…and act upon.

—— Joy: making the most of every day.

—— Let go of the little, petty stuff!

—— For some, it may appear that their compass can't find "North"….or that they can't find their compass.

—— The distance between people, may be those living within the same home.

—— A "G.P.S." can be great; hearing the words: "re-calculating" is not.

—— The outcry from those who view judicial injustice often becomes: follow the power; follow the money.

—— Always, an abundance of poverty prevails!

—— Did you ever time, how many minutes are taken up by commercials, during an "hour-long show"?

—— Just taking another approach to a problem can sometimes mean its solution.

—— Beware what may appear to be "obvious."

—— We're now bombarded with services regarding:
T.V., internet, weight loss, beauty aids, funerals,
etc., etc., etc.

—— We can always find something to worry about.

—— No one is infallible.

—— "Trying to keep up with our technology" creates an
automatic, consumer market.

—— The Olympics: a brief, but important proof, that
man can rise above, even human expectations.

—— "Experience" can never be denied.

—— "Tenacious" can easily meld into "obsessive."

—— The influence of heredity is undeniable.

—— Throughout life, our cries of "…what if?" are
unceasing.

—— A crowd can be the strength or the downfall of the person or object it targets.

—— People can become united. Proof? Watch the thousands of fans in sports arenas.

—— We can never be totally sure of a so-called "sure thing."

—— "Surprises": unexpected, unpredictable, unstoppable.

—— The Universe demands balance: injustice demands justice.

—— The "doer" and the "fixer," if not well guided, can become the loser.

—— Those with little self-esteem become easy victims for abuse.

—— "Too much" easily becomes the element in one's downfall.

—— Mere aging can easily make us feel like we're not in step with the music.

———   Treat each day like walking the beach — each day we're provided clear sand for new footprints.

———   "Second thoughts" are often the saving-grace for incorrect, initial thoughts.

———   A tee-shirt once held the words: "life is fragile. Handle with prayer." (I bought it).

———   Words, like all weapons, have the power to destroy.

———   Our busyness, alone, should keep us busy enough.

———   "New and improved" — a strong statement, frequently used by advertisers. "New and improved" — an even stronger affirmation, if true of our lives.

———   Fear is quite frequently seen as man's greatest threat to happiness.

———   If still alive, there's still time!

———   "Giving" can trigger a plethora of excuses.

———   Death can be viewed as an end or an entrance.

—— Most seniors live on "fixed incomes" — settling on the essentials and passing up the extras.

—— The salaries of many athletes are unfathomable to most Americans.

—— When it comes to "the inevitable," our best choice is to make peace.

—— At times, enthusiasm blinds our reason.

—— Just thinking, about the cost of health care can make many people sick.

—— Destructive lies exact a high price: the mind's peace and the body's health…sooner or later.

—— A key to all undertaking is readiness.

—— You've become master of yourself, when you can remain calm and patient — no matter what happens.

—— "A fresh start": when we can release all the hindrances, the past imperfections of others — and the hurt and remorse in ourselves.

—— Don't waste today, by re-living yesterday's pain and unresolved circumstances.

—— In the end, our greatest peace can come in knowing that we've "Fought the Good Fight."

—— Many people attest to the belief that making a difference in someone else's life can be the best way of making a difference in their own.

—— "Achievement" might not always mean "Success."

—— "Deep Seated Trust": truly believing, at all times, that "all is well."

—— We're now very socially connected….but not necessarily emotionally connected.

—— Our "sudden blow-ups", more likely, are days, months, years — in the making.

—— Still, the human brain continues to be both miraculous and mysterious.

—— Man never has the last word in real, Final Justice.

—— Universal Law has a miraculous power of correcting man's indiscretions and foibles.

—— Beware: persons who refuse to find a single, redeeming feature in their adversaries.

—— "Good" may ultimately win — but, it's frustrating, that it's often in no great hurry.

—— We actually create harmony (or disharmony) in all we think, say, and do.

—— Courage may skip a generation...or more.

—— Kindness, in even the smallest dosage, can prove to be the best medicine.

—— Meanness: retaliation of the cowardly.

—— Truth: the first, important step in becoming free.

—— It would appear that "a sense of style" is not of universal agreement.

—— Truth: not a welcome revelation to those who have painstakingly worked to cover it up.

—— Generally speaking, "looking the other way" usually isn't a positive maneuver.

—— There are those whose lives are lived "only when the cameras are rolling."

—— In the most positive sense: people need people.

—— Live life! Don't just "let it happen!"

—— Never Forget: you get to choose the thoughts you think!

—— At any given time, our "want list" is usually greater than our "need list."

—— Our sense of compassion and kindness may best increase, after experiencing similar circumstances, for which we were once so critical.

—— Be it in our Judicial or Political arenas, money and influence still weigh heavily.

—— Too many hard-working Americans find it virtually impossible to significantly rise above their present state.

—— Too many people view America as a "Land of the Rich" and "Home of the Powerful."

—— Language is usually best served when it's simple and direct.

—— "Ranting and raving" are seldom our best, rhetorical choices.

—— In healthy proportion, being somewhat skeptical can be a protective and needed stance.

—— Some, unfortunately, "do battle with life," at every turn.

—— The "State of our Being" is precarious, if based on our fluctuating circumstances.

—— Sustained contentment comes more from inward peace, not just outward satisfaction….as proven through time.

—— Our only choice toward a situation may be in taking a different approach.

——— "You can't do something about something you can't do something about."

——— Our joy and peace are greatly determined by our response(s) to life.

——— Things like envy, frustration, and worry just corrode the Soul.

——— One sure means toward frustration: not being able to vindicate oneself.

——— Trying to impress people aways requires some portion of our own freedom.

——— Proven ways to gain "internal frustration": stay angry at people, gossip about people, shut people out of your life.

——— Proven ways to gain "internal ease"; be good to people, believe the best, let go of worry and fear.

——— "Attitude" — an inward feeling, evidenced by an outward behavior.

—— One of life's greatest opportunities is to give and to receive love.

—— We generally give our attention to what we love the most.

—— Not rarely, our greatest fears and worries become intensified at night.

—— "Caution" is perhaps our best position, when giving or taking advise.

—— We now have greater access to information — though not always provable, testable, or credible.

—— Hang on! So often, we give up, just prior to seeing our victory.

—— We become a true "victim," when we've decided to embrace and live the title.

—— The truth generally lies just beneath the "glint and the glitter."

—— Not all those in authority are worthy of the title.

—— People appear to wear virtually anything that can be written on a shirt.

—— "Shame" becomes the legacy of guilt.

—— There's still so much we can enjoy in this world!

—— Our criticisms are often born from our hurts.

—— Worry is worthless.

—— It's the application of knowledge, not its mere possession, that gives it worth.

—— One of the worst forms of corruption is accepting corruption.

—— Simply put: quit thinking and talking about it — clean out those closets!

—— Unworn clothes claim yards of hanger space.

—— Public service should be viewed as a "privilege," not as a "passage" to future, personal goals.

—— Definitely futile: trying to right, all perceived wrongs.

—— To whine and complain are not chosen role-models to be passed on.

—— How soon we can ruin another's reputation! How sad!

—— No one is exempt: we all teach....just by the way we live.

—— Some people join virtually everything being proposed.

—— Courage comes with many faces and in many forms.

—— At times, our greatest show of love is allowing those we love, to fail.

—— In reality, gray hair usually indicates the aging process, but not necessarily the maturing process.

—— Love it when stores stress "how much you've saved." Note: would have saved 100%, if declining the trip.

—— There comes a time when thinking about and reading about should materialize in "doing about."

—— It's been said that if the format of democracy doesn't, at times, laugh at itself, it will someday die from rigidity. (Such is also true of its individuals).

—— Generally, a picture or photo can speak volumes.

—— Scandal and politics are repetitiously joined as closely as Siamese twins.

—— Beware: those who, directly or indirectly, ask others to suspend logical belief.

—— Our character becomes our destiny, unless altered.

—— Pain is not meant to be man's permanent state.

—— One feature of a life well-lived: helps the "little person" demonstrate a viable, needed voice.

—— A test for the Soul: neither immediate nor ultimate greed is directing one's personal motivation.

—— Our energies should be driven by ideals, not just by a lucrative gain.

—— Gaining knowledge involves the awareness of many points of view, then finding where the truth actually resides.

—— Insight is a stepping-stone to wisdom…and vice versa.

—— "Un-truths" have power, on the supposition (or gamble) that people won't take the time to discover the "real truth."

—— Man loses hope, most often, when its basis goes no higher, than man.

—— It's truly overwhelming, how many schemes there are with one, common objective: "how to get someone's money."

—— There's always someone out there helping you….to get into debt.

—— Stop and study just how much "money borrowed" will ultimately cost you.

—— Man's mere existence is a testament to the strength of the Human Spirit.

—— Want to feel dumb? Try to identify the "ingredients" listed in nearly all of the products you're using.

—— Paying in cash is becoming an archaic scene.

—— The mouth says: "I can't recall." The heart says: "that's a lie."

—— Ongoing aggravations exact a heavy toll.

—— Excuses only rationalize mistakes.

—— "Gain(s)" can become a highly debatable topic.

—— "Reconciliation," if worthy, entails change.

—— When still, how angelic most children appear… when still.

—— "Late" becomes the identifying feature of some.

—— "Responsibility" loses its luster, when having to be forced.

—— "Emergencies," when (if) defined, can become highly argumentative.

—— Too often, "money" becomes the ultimate and only goal.

—— It's been said that before you criticize....wait, and before you pray...forgive.

—— So much never reaches fruition, when we choose to rush, instead of wait.

—— The best way to live life at any age is to continually find ways that give life meaning.

—— It's hardly fair to ask others to do what we're unwilling to do ourselves.

—— Oh, the prejudice and bigotry! Oh, the evasion and denial!

—— There are times in life, when each of us must stand alone.

———   Somewhere between believing nothing you read in a newspaper, and believing everything you read — the truth may actually exist.

———   "Ego" normally finds it difficult to be "a team player."

———   Parents' aspirations are not always embraced by their offspring.

———   Parents' solutions are not always embraced by their offspring.

———   Some individuals appear to be on a permanent break from rational thinking.

———   What's worse than not knowing what's going on? Probably, not caring what's going on.

———   "Pay attention," (although horrendously over-used by educators), still holds a very credible message.

———   Unconditional love allows room for mistakes…and possible growth.

———   Gratitude is happiness (and vice versa).

—— Most of our break-throughs come during a time of change and facing the unknown.

—— A perspective of "It's always been that way," paves the way for "It will always stay that way."

—— Conditional love is a controlling love.

—— Conditional love generally is a selfish love.

—— Negative glances can be worse than negative comments.

—— Unfortunately, being highly educated provides no particular edge toward successful, human relationships.

—— A home that feels "empty" has little to do with the amount or content of its furnishings.

—— We, ourselves, are the best judge, of what satisfies our Soul.

—— Along our quest for happiness and fulfillment, we may receive many passionate, though ill-informed means of advice.

—— Happiness comes from changing our inner conditions, not necessarily our outer circumstances.

—— The best kind of unconditional love is what we're willing to give ourselves.

—— Self-criticism and rejection easily become self-fulfillment.

—— It becomes a healthier opinion to believe that we are inherently whole and worthy.

—— Science focuses on the evolution of the body; spirituality focuses on the evolution of the Spirit.

—— Our awareness defines our reality.

—— The aging process is often demonstrated, when our sentiments are basically those of our parents.

—— Even while lending a hand of compassion, it's important to maintain the strength of understanding.

—— Periodically, it's important to re-evaluate our dependence on the people and things in our life.

—— A lack of self-discipline seldom brings positive results.

—— Just waking up in the morning is a miracle! (Especially, or possibly, remembering how you went to bed!)

—— Ever get those little snippets of childhood reverie?

—— Pessimism is the death-blow to possibility.

—— No one goes through life un-scathed!

—— Have you ever felt that you can't believe what you're hearing?

—— Relaxation is the prerequisite, if you're ever going to have peace and healing.

—— When your view of life is "whatever," life's response to you is "whatever."

—— It's also been said that money is a wonderful servant, but a terrible master.

——— "Civilization" and "civilized" have had a history of ongoing (and debatable) meanings.

——— So very many have embraced, and hold on to the philosophy that: "it's all about money."

——— Wisdom has value when it's used…and future value….when it's passed on.

——— No relationship comes with a guarantee.

——— Somewhere between "compulsive" and "passive" lies an area for the possibility of "normal."

——— Too much of life has become a battleground — with weapons too easily available as a response.

——— Ongoing peace may require ongoing patience.

——— "Mail": knows many faces; elation, contempt, anxiety, confusion, dread, impatience, regret, etc., etc., etc.

——— Some have, skillfully mastered words and their power to manipulate.

—— Man's "inward bruises", more often than not,
surprisingly take far longer to heal.

—— Today, we seem to be involved in continual combat:
with family, friends, government, foreign countries,
etc.

—— Sometimes, the greater weakness lies in not
knowing when to give up, than in just giving up.

—— There is a distinction between the scholar and the
innovator.

—— Many pets act a lot more patient than their owners.

—— One of the best legacies we can leave behind is:
what it feels like to be loved.

—— "Crutches" (not those manufactured and sold) easily
become a way of not facing problems head-on.

—— Saying "I was wrong" — is like speaking a foreign
language to some.

—— Sometimes, everyone around you sounds dumb.

——— Endurance — having the Faith to wait.

——— Peace — enduring the wait with Faith.

——— Our deeds — good or bad — always find a way to exact recompense.

——— Few are as smart as they think they are. Sometimes, we give too much credit to the undeserving.

——— Trying to decide our best choice, when dealing opposing positions? Listen carefully to their opposing answers.

——— Being biased is one of the best ways of staying ignorant.

——— Those who are prejudiced will virtually never allow that term as an identification.

——— Defending those who are wrong always proves a loss.

——— Those models parading on high-fashion runways compare little to the common man....in gait, expression, or attire.

—— Sometimes it seems like an eternity before we see justice....but it's always worth the wait.

—— Politicians: far too often, demonstrate the worst of childhood; exaggerated truths and ongoing ramblings.

—— The only things worth accumulating while you're alive are those things you can take with you when you die.

—— No teaching is worth anything, unless it's believed and applied.

—— Every part of our mind and body that is knowingly abused will, at some point, be heard.

—— There are those who go through life, never accepting that people are different. They're among the unhappy ones.

—— Our world has increasingly become a more fearful, cynical, and combative state.

—— Oh, how we can "spin" the English language!

——— Some handle money, the way they handle people — very carelessly/ then wonder where it, or they, have gone.

——— Injustice ruins lives.

——— In the hands of the honest, money has a real chance to do good.

——— Man's laws will always be fallible, since they're made and enforced by man…who is fallible.

——— A barometer of one's maturity can be evidenced by the degree of one's patience.

——— It's bad when some can't find anywhere to rest. It's even worse when some simply can't rest.

——— There are those who are ready to "do," but never know what it is to just "be."

——— Those who are wise know that life is not immune to difficulty; yet difficulty can sometimes lead to peace.

——— We have to unceasingly refuse to be downcast!

—— At times, the heart hears clearer than the ears.

—— Do weapons usually ensure and bring justice?

—— A prevalent affirmation holds to the belief that it's not life and its difficulties that we must conquer, but rather ourselves.

—— Many of man's indiscretions have been solely attributed to the need of perseverance.

—— In some way, at some time, life does demonstrate that sacrifice and suffering can be redemptive.

—— The value of each life can be subjective.

—— The only thing worse than accepting everything — is denying everything.

—— The word "gift" is open to a variety of connotations.

—— Rest only comes when we cease all struggle — both mental and physical.

—— Don't be too easily satisfied...or dissatisfied.

—— Real love tries to find good, even in the dull, the uninteresting, the critical, and the clueless.

—— The unspoken word can have greater power than the spoken word.

—— Remember: how many "never(s)" have been disproven.

—— Simplicity is often the most difficult course of action.

—— Our strength is very often dictated by our enthusiasm and desire.

—— The length and breadth of our happiness is determined by its source and validity.

—— Grumpy and complaining are not the best choices in starting a new day.

—— Our excuses just keep us deceived!

—— People who speak unceasingly and hastily are very often ill advised.

—— It's much better to have kindness in your heart than a Christian Bumper Sticker on your car.

—— "Screaming," "ranting," and "raving" have become common-place reactions of more and more people.

—— Warning: when you can't seem to dislodge all worry, fear, anxiety — at any given time.

—— Some look for easy things to do, instead of tackling the hard things. Even worse: some look for nothing to do.

—— "Passivity" robs all potential and possible success.

—— How often we get upset about things that never happen!

—— Flash: sometimes we just have to learn how to get along with people!

—— Many have discovered that when they change in a positive, stable, and permanent way, it almost always promotes some change in those around them.

—— Beware of the many ways we're set up to get upset.

—— Brokenness comes when we learn that we have a lot to learn.

—— It's often been declared that brokenness leads to humility, and humility precedes honor.

—— It's also been said that "haughtiness" (pride) comes before disaster. (Seen all too often).

—— Temptation never ends.

—— Some people only see "differences," as "wrongs."

—— If you need to apologize, do it! Now!

—— Constantly dragging our old, hurtful memories leaves little strength in making newer, better ones.

—— A sure way to remain constantly unhappy is taking your flaws too seriously, and constantly obsessing over them.

—— Enjoy yourself, and lighten up!

——— Don't constantly dread. When dread enters, joy leaves.

——— According to our mindset, we can dictate our Heaven or our Hell.

——— A person who doesn't trust, dreads life and fears people.

——— Nothing can drain us so quickly of our energy as emotional trauma.

——— Ultimate contentment is not found in places, people, or situations.

——— We become what we're determined to be….no more and no less.

——— The best way to do nothing is to associate with those who have this very goal.

——— "Happiness" has many meanings.

——— Perseverance is needed, even when the world is viewed as a sad and confusing place.

—— At times, we just have to learn how to be grateful.

—— It really does become a real balancing act in trying to juggle a family and a career.

—— We're really blessed when we help, just for the sake of helping, based on no financial gain.

—— It sometimes takes real courage to say, "I don't know."

—— The body and mind's power of renewal is truly miraculous.

—— There really is a beauty in every season — in Nature and in Life.

—— Most people long for a better world. Some people make it happen.

—— Nearly everyone holds certain hurts — known or unknown to those around them.

—— If not careful, the world can easily harden our heart.

—— At times, we need strength to bear the burden of love.

—— Seemingly miraculous is how we can manage to have the right words, at the right time.

—— A fickle nature makes a dangerous friend.

—— It's actually a gift, in learning how to grieve our losses.

—— Our choices become our destiny.

—— Selfish ego: another human attribute, not to be nurtured.

—— Having no purpose in life is an intentional disregard of all of one's talents.

—— Flash: we don't always get to do things "our way."

—— Life often teaches: "be still and know….one thing at a time!"

—— Most people want to believe that what they do matters.

———   Want to know true peace?...Forgive.

———   There's wisdom in knowing when to fight — and when to stop fighting.

———   Spring: a constant reminder in the Power of Life's rebirth and renewal.

———   A good motto: to be anxious in saying something nice….and in keeping the not-so-nice things to oneself.

———   To not be afraid of "loss" is difficult to overcome.

———   Keeping "life-long friends" is a true accomplishment.

———   It takes real courage to love without fear.

———   There are always more things with value and meaning, beyond what you see today.

———   It has been charged that those who abuse their body have little respect for creation.

———   Some people just refuse "to step out of the way."

—— It's easy to have (or allow) the busyness, the messiness, or the heaviness of life to consume us.

—— At best, at any given time, we never see or know "the Big Picture."

—— Emotion sometimes appears as our chief source of consciousness.

—— Doing things quickly often means….not doing them thoroughly.

—— Never be so busy teaching that you have no time to learn.

—— Experience gives life to ideas.

—— Words often fail to capture the effect that music has on us.

—— Pretense has no earthly value, to either its bearer or its recipient.

—— Purpose: the kind of person you want to be, and the kind of life you want to live.

—— Many see success in the "doing," not just in the "getting."

—— A set-back can be a chance for a come-back.

—— More people ask for advice, than are willing to take it.

—— We can usually learn more from what people do, than what they say.

—— It's very difficult to achieve very much, if you're extremely quiet and passive.

—— A sense of humor helps in both labor and leadership situations.

—— There are those who would generally prefer the "legend and myth" to the "fact and truth."

—— It appears that there will always be the necessity for work.

—— Champions traditionally radiate a will that is even stronger than the skill.

—— Too often, we give all our enemies the ideas and means toward our own destruction.

—— Courage, in some form, is demanded every day.

—— We lose the blessing of any entity, when we begin to take it for granted.

—— All the people in our life can help us to discover who we are.

—— Even the smallest bit of Faith can work wonders.

—— It may take a lifetime to learn one of life's greatest lessons: "what matters most."

—— Many families are tested with a unique personality type: "….the opinionated-know-it-all."

—— Beware: when you cannot be happy, unless surrounded by an entourage, or in a crowd of people.

—— Blessings: those in life who have helped us carry our burdens.

—— Our inner vision will determine our outer accomplishment.

—— Thank Heaven, our pets have no real frame of reference for the names they're given.

—— The victory of others is able to inspire us in what we can accomplish.

—— Good communication is one of the best roads to peace.

—— How much do arguments usually solve?

—— "Expectation," if positive, is just another word for "hope."

—— Frequently, life's timing is not on our schedule.

—— Most of our tangled messes are our own making.

—— The "impossible" can sometimes be mastered, a little at a time.

—— Never confuse what's easy, with what's right!

—— Too many opinions! Too few facts!

—— A person must embody peace, before its effect can promote peace in others.

—— Our children don't come with any type of guarantee.

—— People frequently need reassurance throughout life; however, it can't always be provided.

—— There are those who frequently blame "a poor start" for their ongoing, present problems.

—— How sad! That so many choose to direct their exceptional talents toward destructive agendas.

—— Perhaps one advantage of aging is having more time and insight to appreciate and enjoy what's really important.

—— You never run away from yourself!

—— The present is what's "in season"!

——— We can't experience inner stillness, until we learn how to periodically turn away from the chatter of the external world.

——— Most people have more creative power than they ever use.

——— Peace is promoted by our calm thoughts, words of conciliation, and constructive action.

——— Did you ever….not understand what you were looking at….but, you couldn't look away?

——— Life has a way of tripping us up….at other times, we have a way of tripping ourselves up.

——— It has been stated that pain may be part of life, but suffering is optional.

——— Periodically, we get unexpected blessings from unexpected channels.

——— Every living being may appear to have an inner compass — but not everyone appears to use it.

—— Honor is established, when we honor our commitments.

—— Too often, people only apologize after being caught or embarrassed. (Does that count?)

—— Being positive or negative is contagious. Oftentimes, the negative seems to be even more contagious.

—— Troubled minds often initiate troubling situations.

—— When we focus on lack, life often fulfills it.

—— At times, non-resistance can actually be the best strategy in getting around obstacles.

—— Inner strength is often the motivating force that materializes into outer strength.

—— Feeling overwhelmed by continuous demands is the everyday mind-set of too many people.

—— Why is this happening? — We might not get any answers. What can I do? — We might get some suggestions.

——— "Understanding," helps build strong bridges toward better relationships.

——— "Predictable" certainly is not always an appropriate adjective when describing "Life."

——— "Competition" has been an ongoing activity of man, since the annals of time.

——— Competition: tells much about the character of the person who wins....and the person who loses.

——— What inspires some...may repulse others.

——— Some refuse to believe what they actually see!

——— There are those who believe that generosity is actually encoded in our DNA.

——— Evidence exists that love does have the power to both heal and restore.

——— At times, the only thing an elderly person needs (and wants) is someone to talk to.

—— Kindness and compassion are never wasted — even when rejected by others, they're a blessing to oneself.

—— National pride really does run deep!

—— A life can be changed by one, defining instant of inspiration.

—— Goal: as humans, we're to grow "inwardly"…not just "outwardly."

—— Denial is not necessarily bad — but certainly bad, if denying the truth.

—— We can't always give another person Faith and Hope.

—— We can easily take, however, Faith and Hope from another person.

—— Belief gives birth to potential.

—— The number of things we postpone can easily correlate with the number of regrets we create.

——   Many who believe in Heaven, view it, not as a future destination, but as a present reality.

——   A strong affirmation proclaims that neither space nor time can separate a person from his good.

——   Everyone needs guidance at some point in life.

——   Just because something was not part of our past, doesn't mean it can't be part of our future.

——   Thoughts of doubt and insecurity are just remnants of old thinking that can obscure one's total outlook.

——   Watch out for those people who live, only to gain credit, publicity, or notoriety.

——   Life has to be lived day by day!

——   Life has to be lived moment by moment!

——   Compassion always trumps hurried judgement.

——   You can give and not love, but you can't love, and not give.

—— Some people hang an invisible life-sign on themselves which reads: "do not disturb."

—— "Demonstrating" can add power and depth to "believing."

—— Personal retreats help provide solace, refreshment, and renewal, from the stresses of life.

—— As documented, too many lives are lost with weapons in the hands of the uneducated and unscrupulous.

—— There's always delicate balance that's needed to co-exist peacefully.

—— "Things that happen in you" are more important than "things that happen around you."

—— A must: letting go of "the weight of the world" — as soon as possible.

—— It's questionable how many people know what they're doing, even some of the time.

——— Futility: believing (and practicing) that we have the answers to other peoples' lives.

——— Freedom: demonstrating that I don't have to be bound by my past actions or beliefs.

——— Man's power: to make amends, correct one's errors, and to forgive.

——— When we're alone, our fears and hurts become more intensified, and seemingly, less likely to be resolved.

——— Life comes with gifts and challenges!

——— There's an inexplicable value in the beauty of togetherness, companionship, and connection.

——— "Wish lists" can be a very positive move, if including strategies toward their accomplishment.

——— Our world cannot be based solely on "our" needs.

——— Many aren't as self-confident as they appear.

—— Powerful, positive thoughts lead to powerful, positive outcomes.

—— Be aware of time! One day, you'll see just how fast it really went!

—— We actually do live in a world of infinite possibilities.

—— Note: every Faith tradition has stories about the exchange of gifts.

—— We can be grateful for both all the love we've experienced, and all the love we have to share.

—— Ultimately, an enormous level of personal growth is being grateful for lessons taught, even by one's abusers.

—— Peace of mind is a foundation in maintaining health within the physical body.

—— An irritated person spawns an irritated environment.

—— Frustration: never feeling you have enough time, energy, or patience to accomplish what needs to be done.

—— Never become a victim of other people's intentions!

—— There will always be circumstances that allow no pre-preparation.

—— A healthy outlook sees every day as a new beginning.

—— Justice can be won or lost, depending on the skill or ineptness of the lawyers involved.

—— If mathematically calculated, some of those diet ads can have you at your pre-teen weight in a matter of weeks.

—— In retrospect, delays can be seen as blessings.

—— Delay is not denial!

—— What we choose to absorb…we radiate.

—— Our own spirits can easily become weighed down, if we continually obsess on the faults and sorrows around us.

—— The most taxing and difficult pressures we put on ourselves are often the most difficult to alleviate.

—— Not all relation-breakups are to be mourned.

—— It's self-infliction to pursue problems that we just can't solve.

—— To proclaim: "don't be afraid" usually has little impact.

—— Too many in powerful positions take advantage of the misinformation and lack of knowledge of the masses.

—— It takes real courage to stand apart from the world.

—— It's unbelievable how goofy some people act...yet survive.

—— The parade of temptations throughout life offers no promise of our eventual success in dealing with any of them.

—— Some foods become more edible, if not viewed.

—— Good intentions are worlds apart from good actions.

—— "Relevance," in any undertaking, can never be down-played.

—— When looking more closely, some losses may be seen as ultimate blessings.

—— People shouldn't have to become desperate, before help is offered.

—— Bluntly put: life without purpose is vanity.

—— After all the dust clears, the greatest thing in the world is still love.

—— Suffering, very often, can be a prelude to reward.

—— Being patient with those who have intentionally hurt us isn't easy.

—— Why does it invariably cost even more than usually anticipated?

—— "Keeping records" is commendable as a business practice, but not necessarily in human relationships.

—— Though unintentionally, we can enable others to mistreat or abuse us.

—— Too many times, we're sure that someone else is the problem.

—— For many, blaming someone else has become their automatic, reactive response.

—— Our behavior virtually has some effect on everyone around us.

—— The seat of our happiness and unhappiness lies within ourselves.

—— Spoiled people manage to spoil their own lives.

—— Some are quick to correct nearly everyone.

—— Man immediately realizes how little control he has, when Mother Nature immediately takes over.

—— It's alright to question, but not to hold unshakable, pre-conceived answers.

—— Cruelty to animals is unconscionable and cowardly.

—— When we're too weak to care, a part of our life has already been surrendered.

—— Some theorists propose that all of man's experiences — even the (seemingly) most insignificant — play a part in man's ultimate destiny.

—— Time may be the missing ingredient in man's understanding.

—— Why do so many people gravitate to garage sales — with no initial goal in mind?

—— Words!...Words!...Words!....Our solace, our power....our fear, our downfall.

—— As in their lives, some clean their homes: with anything objectionable being "swept under the rug."

—— There are times when we just have to "bite our tongue."

—— In time, most learn the lesson, of not "biting one's tongue."

—— Americans have become increasingly dissatisfied with their Representatives in Congress.

—— Americans have become increasingly frustrated with how the disfunction in Congress has grown.

—— Creating doubt is one of man's most lethal maneuvers in covering up the truth.

—— One of the greatest barriers to Faith is doubt.

—— Animals habitually demonstrate as having more brains than humans.

—— "Attempting to do" is still more reputable than "avoiding to do"....but neither is as good as "succeeding to do."

—— So many demonstrate that "look of disbelief," when convicted of disregarding those large, publicly displayed warning signs.

—— Some people simply can't (or refuse to) hear anyone else's voice other than their own.

—— After living with someone a life-time, we've almost gathered a storehouse of information…almost.

—— Taking medicines become serious decisions….but how about those side-effects? Even more decisions!

—— Many people appear shocked, after receiving their medial report. If being honest, most can easily relate their lifestyles to the findings.

—— There are few "absolutes," as proposed by man.

—— Watch what you're watching — it's effect can keep you confused, give you clarity, cause you anger, or even lighten your spirits.

—— Judgement has the distinct disadvantage in not having the complete picture of another's total reality.

—— One of the worst things to short-change is your health.

—— The hypochondriac is able to translate any and all possible symptoms into any and all probable, or fatal diagnoses.

—— Deciding what's "fair" can, itself, become the battleground of turmoil. Remember: a "guess" is just that…a guess.

—— Music defines each, subsequent generation.

—— Unfortunately, justification can often be based only on a very personal frame of reference.

—— When anxiously waiting, time seems to barely move at all.

—— Our "what if's" play a horrendous role in constantly robbing our lives of peace and happiness.

—— Weight Gain: when virtually all our cravings are honored. Weight Loss: when virtually all our cravings are denied.

——— Sudden disaster is a test of personal co-operation, preparation, and endurance.

——— Some have little respect for life, best shown by their responses to it.

——— Life has an astounding way of exacting its measure of justice….its pound of flesh.

——— If words are ghosts, there's real validity that there will be a haunting.

——— Those, who have really lost their way, see their futures as either: in a hospital, prison, or grave.

——— "To die for" is much safer, as a flippant outburst of preference, than a serious proclamation of action.

——— True friendship is tested many times, and on many levels and stages.

——— Some of our greatest accomplishments are made, not in segments of miles…but in inches.

——— "To demonstrate" becomes the proof of what was once, merely "to claim."

—— It's true that life marches on. It's also unpreventably true that each, older generation must hand over the baton to the next generation.

—— Since no one is perfect, any perspective foe can easily find some flaw to expose, if desired.

—— "Nerves" can spoil the outcome of nearly everything that man can hope to achieve.

—— Those who deny the ongoing problem of racism are either oblivious, or hope others are.

—— How successful our war on drugs has been continues to be an ongoing debate.

—— Some hide from work….some work to hide.

—— Why does everything look better, when the sun comes out?

—— If the vast majority in Congress is getting such low marks, why are so many "returning as members"?

—— How many of us would opt to relive our childhood years?

———   No matter the topic, it's almost inevitable to see two, opposing sides take shape.

———   Oh, how we make excuses for our children! Oh, how we usually live to regret it!

———   We're often much more patient in instructing other people's children, than our own.

———   It's astounding, how many things we dread, either before, during or after their completion.

———   Man's Downfall: that we simply choose to think.... what we weren't meant to think.

———   Man's Downfall: that we simply choose to do.... what we weren't meant to do.

———   Parental skill does not mean that you can invariably locate all your missing children by the end of every outing.

———   If, at the onset of a challenge, you say that you'll never win...you probably won't.

—— When promises stop at "the verbal stage," they've died a premature death.

—— You never want to be at "another person's mercy."

—— Bluntly stated: there are tons of drivers who should never have been given a license.

—— For many of the elderly, moving in with their children becomes life's final hurdle.

—— "Dumb" crosses all blood, cultural, and financial lines.

—— Few people are anxious to hear the truth about themselves.

—— Our fear is too often our reason for postponing any medical confrontations.

—— "Weird" also appears to be quite democratic — crossing over lines of ethnicity, age, and gender.

—— Real tragedy: if the "buck for justice" really stopped with man.

—— How bored we'd soon be, if we could automatically have all we asked for.

—— How often our Faith is tested. How often, we fail its test.

—— There are times, when it seems that we don't have a choice....and that becomes our choice.

—— It's only when we remove all the make-up that we see what really exists.

—— There are things that man just can't improve upon.

—— "Choice" is one of the greatest privileges and dangers that we have.

—— Vengeance can be in the form of boisterous attack to quiet subtlety.

—— Our outward appearance should never become the primary detriment for our failure.

—— Take a lesson from flowers: they just bloom where they're planted and offer joy indiscriminately.

—— When man must battle Mother Nature, the outcome is usually predictable.

—— The "selfish" only end up with "self."

—— Some people, like time, appear to be unstoppable.

—— If your closet is sporting lots of clothes, many with tags on them, it might be good to either wear them, or give them away.

—— Our goals can easily become our obsessions.

—— Waiting to buy gas, when running on fumes — isn't good timing for our vehicles...or our lives.

—— A person's outward stride can be very indicative of one's inward pace.

—— Many of us would like to think that we're as smart as we think we are.

—— Our weakness lies in being frustrated with the Untruth. Our strength comes in knowing the Truth.

—— The value of someone's word is how well that word materializes.

—— The world can seem cruel — still, we create many of our own indiscretions.

—— Faith doesn't insulate us from having problems, but Faith provides the power to face them.

—— Our mindset embodies our perspective toward our problems, allowing us to succeed, or at worst, to endure.

—— Beware: when saturated in a feeling of desperation, nothing looks hopeful or possible.

—— Beware: habitually going through life, worrying; "what's going to happen next"?

—— Everyone, everyone….has limitations and weaknesses.

—— Ironically discovering our strengths, often comes after recognizing our weaknesses.

—— Basically, our lives are defined by how we interact with other lives.

—— It's only when our automatic, bodily systems fail, that we truly come to appreciate them.

—— Finally, we decide to change, when there's no other choice.

—— It's not rare that an "after-thought" turns out to be the "better thought."

—— Time appears to answer to no one.

—— In some instances, life just doesn't provide us with a second chance.

—— How we handle defeat dictates how soon we begin again…to live.

—— The fewer our interests, the fewer our chances of living a full life.

—— Fixed incomes are simply at the mercy of rising costs.

—— The aged often look at life as having fewer surprises but providing greater understanding.

—— "Intended to" or "meant to" easily becomes translated as "failed to."

—— "I will never…." is an easy set-up in becoming a failed sentiment.

—— Our focus gives direction to our energies.

—— Our present circumstance, (in retrospect), becomes a "season."

—— To recognize is alright; to dwell on, usually, is not.

—— Knowing what to resist is a start. Resisting what we know is the better.

—— Our unhappiness usually comes from focusing on what we want, not on what we have.

—— "Give credit, where credit is due" has been an age-old affirmation.

—— "OUR" lives are just that — not to be given to, or lived for, anyone else.

—— Be aware of those who build you up, not beat you up.

—— It can become dangerous to give people a foothold — which can then, easily become a stronghold.

—— Live your life — not just in asking "Why"? Live your life in also asking — "Why not"?

—— Some things just can't be promised.

—— We all need moments to stop and celebrate.

—— Most people have done things that even surprised them.

—— We celebrate life when we take time to acknowledge our heart-felt gratitude.

—— A simple rule of life: the less fault-finding, the more enjoyment.

—— "To sell out" goes beyond what we should ever be willing to sell.

—— Our sensitivity can open the door to all of life's heartaches….but also, all of life's joys.

—— Perseverance can be its own, greatest reward.

—— To never fail would mean to never grow.

—— Our body and mind can endure a great deal of neglect, before signs of illness and breakdown.

—— Man's poor decisions are often righted, with time.

—— If you want to waste a portion of your financial gain, begin purchasing the constant, numerous products continuously advertised.

—— Feeling sorry for yourself? Visit a Children's Cancer Center, Wounded Warrior's Hospital, etc.

—— Sadly, it's only after we experience a physical or mental malady that our compassion begins to grow.

—— Faith is more than believing that God can. It is knowing that God will!

—— It's also been stated that compromise can be viewed as going just below what you know is right.

—— Very often, those who are the source of the problem — are also the source of the solution.

—— Many times, things must get worse, before they can begin to get better.

—— Some of the best things we're able to give away are free.

—— At times, the best we can do in life is "to manage."

—— Whether we hope to, or even realize, because we all die, we all leave a legacy.

—— It's not just a question of "Will it happen"? It's more likely a question of "When will it happen"?

—— Some of our greatest warriors have never touched a gun.

—— At times, the choice and the question becomes: how can I avoid? or….How can I help?

—— If worry is your strong suit, you can play it every day — but never expect to be a winner.

—— Not everyone who disagrees with us, or tries to correct us, is against us.

—— Flash: as you're feverishly yelling, that image on your television screen can't hear you.

—— Even when crucial, apologies to some (if requested) are virtually impossible.

—— Realistically, down-playing the power and influence of money is extremely naïve.

—— There can be a fine line between defending and excusing.

—— Frustration: those envelops, who's backing never has enough glue, are irksome to seal.

—— It's our results, not our promises, that matter.

—— Our views as adults, (not infrequently), become based on the views of those who raised us.

—— Those who are blatantly insensitive to others, can be very sensitive, if they view such treatment is directed toward them.

—— Sell no one short!

—— Ultimately, it's a losing fight to try to out-talk the Truth.

—— Truth wins — one way or another!

—— There simply are times when "money really isn't the issue."

—— There are even more times when "money really is the issue."

—— And then, there are times when the entity known as money may, or may not, be involved.

—— Unfortunately, being uninformed or not particularly knowledgeable has still been known to successfully captivate and sway the masses.

——— After being able to escape a near-catastrophe, the aftermath often allows and motivates a rethinking of our priorities.

——— Flash: our priorities may not be the world's priorities.

——— Things being cancelled can be a disappointment…. or, later seen as a blessing.

——— Some systems are actually designed to fail.

——— From the perspective of our youth, we can always gain new and fresh ideas.

——— Who better to know adversity, than those who have survived, or even benefited from it.

——— Being "outraged" is not necessarily bad — not when such energies can make things better.

——— Subjectivity always opens the door for conflict.

——— Change for the better may be long in coming — but always worth the wait and the time.

—— Little credence is awarded the position: "I can't put my finger on why I feel that way."

—— Our ignorance can be demonstrated most strongly when…we speak.

—— It's mind-boggling how many people boldly appear on T.V. to expose the intimacies of their lives.

—— The factors that influence our life come from a myriad of sources.

—— It's really miraculous how many accidents are narrowly diverted on a daily basis.

—— Some marriages operate like a chess game — each party calculating separately in order to win.

—— Some people appear to be operating with an empty tool box.

—— Unfortunately, man's integrity must sometimes be motivated by fear of ordained consequences.

—— To those who wish to find loopholes in any rhetoric, "vague" is a key.

——— Mistakes are basically choosing the worst, of all existing options at the moments.

——— Not rarely, people have gone to their death, refusing to repeat certain information.

——— "Hard feelings" can become like toxic air we breathe.

——— It's interesting how varied the definition of "stealing" has become.

——— Too much money involved….too many frivolous lawsuits filed.

——— "I'm entitled" is a premise that immediately becomes open for debate.

——— Undeniable: the human race is filled with unrepressed and unstoppable passion.

——— How easily our emotions can be changed, diverted, and justified.

—— "Wrong is not necessarily wrong" — an argument coming from those who wish to extend its boundaries.

—— Few things in man's world are "100%."

—— So many people, who have hearing problems, insist the world is mumbling.

—— "Tolerance" is a beautiful premise, but would be even more beautiful, if consistently followed.

—— When we can't trust, we usually find it hard to commit.

—— Too much….is often just that…too much.

—— "Drive" has frequently been the winning force over "ability."

—— You don't always have to like something, to do it.

—— "Waiting for the opportune time" can often mean waiting for a life time.

—— Not everything is justifiable…maybe not everything.

—— Not everything you like is good for you…no it isn't.

—— "Careless" is an attribute that opens the door to an endless number of problems and frustrations.

—— We can easily be too subjective, when identifying or evaluating our flaws and weaknesses.

—— You know you're in trouble, when even your dog doesn't want to have anything to do with you.

—— Not uncommon: too easily and often praise and hug others, but not so with those in your own family.

—— Members of our population see living as a choice between living life in fear…or full throttle.

—— You're missing something in life, when you're looking forward to going to the dentist.

—— In time, we learn that whenever and wherever possible, our best move is to try to replace what's bad, with something that's better.

——— There are individuals who — no matter the situation or philosophy — have decided to never agree with, or make peace with, the opposing side.

——— Always the hope: the more we're willing to learn about — the more we can understand, appreciate, and agree with.

——— Somehow, man invariably manages to make complicated, even those things, whose original natures are simple.

——— There are those who sort of know, those who almost know, and those who really know.

——— There are also those who sometimes know, those who rarely know, and those who will never know.

——— Even when doing your best, it's important to remember the source of your power.

——— You know you have a problem, when you're the only one in the neighborhood that stray animals flee from.

——— Even the "Doctor's orders" have, on occasion, proven wrong.

—— Usually when sick enough, a hospital gets one's vote.

—— Worse than making a mistake is the refusal to either admit it or change it.

—— "It is what it is"….becomes the take on the present situation. Even if dire, resignation is a useless stance.

—— Wisdom: knowing when we can do something…. what that something is….and when our efforts must stop.

—— Large numbers of people are, in no way, an immediate or credible indicator of knowledge represented.

—— The way a man operates is quite often a fair indicator of his future success and ending.

—— Our real winnings in life are not always intended to produce financial gain.

—— We quite often create our own struggles.

—— Too many who vow "they don't like"….never have tried, been associated with, or even heard of.

—— We never totally escape what we are tirelessly trying to escape.

—— "I wish…." is usually the prélude to the bucket list of our regrets.

—— There are those whose journey is basically a transition from one crisis to another.

—— There isn't a profession that doesn't contain both saints and sinners.

—— Why are some of women's "flimsiest" clothes, the most expensive? (Certainly, not much material involved).

—— Some parents (usually the Moms) were really the ones who should have been awarded those "badges" from certain childhood organizations.

—— No one escapes without trying.

—— No one feels change without believing.

—— Oh, those moments….when there was a frantic need….and no restroom in sight.

—— Although it's no guarantee, being educated in the law seems to have its advantages.

—— Some animals look like their owners (and vice versa).

—— A lot of visitors in a hospital look like they should be admitted.

—— Do you ever wonder just how they manage all those "special effects" in the movies?

—— Listening to some of our politicians, some of them don't even appear as candidates for a high school degree.

—— Listening to some of our seated representatives, it becomes blatantly obvious how out of touch they are with those they're elected to represent.

—— Some never realize how wabbly their self-constructed halos are.

—— It's not uncommon that in some households, it's the pets who call the shots.

—— It's not rare that our physical recovery from many ailments is strongly affected by our mental and emotional state.

—— We become what we believe. We can fail from disbelief.

—— A smile can have many meanings and purposes.

—— Actually, not having a choice does not necessarily make things easier.

—— How about those clothes your Mom dressed you in, when you were young?

—— If anything, our children usually remember where we screwed up with them.

—— Laughter is healing; worry is disabling.

—— Those who grab for too much in life, often have too little to grab onto when life is nearing its end.

—— Just the mere proximity of some individuals sparks an immediate conflict.

—— Some gamble and win. For most, it's a less lucrative outcome.

—— Our lives can mimic the birthing process: progressive, minimal pain, joyous; or; problematic, stressful, and prolonged pain.

—— There are human competitions that beg the question: stupendous skill? or stupidity?

—— One's weight has become an important variable in many, existing, health problems.

—— Often the storms in life come with little or no warning.

—— Whatever the endeavor, always know the risks.

—— Want an immediate lift from your problems? Have an unexpected call from a grandchild.

—— The thought: "nothing lasts forever" may be our only, applicable thought in catastrophic situations.

—— Some victories are even surprises to the victor.

—— If disappointment is never defeated, success has little chance to materialize.

—— The majority of Americans are eating faster, eating unhealthier, and developing more maladies.

—— Cutting certain things out of our lives may be wise. Real wisdom lies in knowing what to cut out….and how to keep them out.

—— "Woe" to the parents who refuse to accept the strengths and weaknesses of their offspring….and a greater "Woe" to the offspring involved.

—— Our transgressions always require a payment.

—— Certain things that are precious to some, have absolutely no value to others.

—— There are those who place virtually everyone else below themselves.

—— Exhaustion: fighting against everyone and everything that we view as different from ourselves.

——— Some welcome a household of guests and entertain with ease; others become anxious, desperate, and exhausted.

——— One's historical background might be best used as a reference, not an indictment.

——— Vulnerability, at least to some degree, appears to be a universal entity.

——— It's interesting how many people vehemently insist that they do not snore.

——— Just listen to what's advertised. There's something for everything that ails you — so they say.

——— Any ultimatum can create an equal amount of anxiety for both parties involved.

——— For most, our memories lose clarity and content with age.

——— "Impossible" is defined differently, depending on who is being asked.

———   Dumb: doing the opposite of what you know is right.

———   Take heart — it can't always be your fault…right?

———   Continuing our child-like ways throughout our adult life defines us as childish.

———   Today, too many hard-working Americans find it seemingly impossible to get out of debt.

———   There are those who ultimately come to see their lives as wasted. In many cases, fortune and glory were their goals.

———   Flash: people in other lands and continents often see us, and our workings, as weird.

———   But for chance of birth, we all could be a different ethnicity, race, and religion.

———   Man is meant to be free — neither a captive, nor owner of a captive.

———   "Clarity" is not always among man's strong points.

—— Keep it simple…keep it honest.

—— Entertainment, to some extent, becomes an essential.

—— It's a form of masochism to continue watching, listening to, or being around what really angers you.

—— For the good or the bad, we can easily become a part of our habitual surroundings.

—— There are things that we just shouldn't be afraid of.

—— Eventually, most begin to realize just how fast their lives are going.

—— In reality, change is most meaningful when it takes place from the inside, not from the outside.

—— It takes a serious and ongoing lifestyle to attain and maintain being healthy, whole, and well.

—— "Eyesight" — one of the most beautiful, wonderous and functional gifts of our human senses.

—— "Feeling out of place" is quite often initiated by others who occupy a place.

—— Stalling is an often-used tactic — merely an extension toward an inevitable conclusion.

—— We can provide our children with many things — but too often, it's not "the things" they need.

—— Like our high school classmates, our views about certain of our teachers will change with time.

—— Is there really anywhere that can earn the title of: "a stress-free environment"?

—— Just when you see life as "not fair"….think about all the things you "luckily got away with."

—— The best way to stay sick is to dwell on every aspect of your illness…constantly.

—— Even when those closest to you say: "I understand completely"…they probably don't.

—— The titles given to certain professions certainly sound impressive…though not necessarily.

——— Being technologically illiterate is modern-day illiteracy.

——— "Careful" is a very relative term.

——— How well: "don't try this at home" is adhered to? Just watch the 6:00 p.m. or 11:00 p.m. news.

——— One of the easiest ways to lose the glee over one's bank account is in receiving a dubious health report.

——— Life changes quickly — a moment of silence becomes a moment of hysteria — in a moment.

——— It's unbelievable how long we put up with chronic, aggravating, health conditions.

——— You have to have a dream! Even a little dream!

——— A stare, met with lowered eyebrow is usually not a good thing.

——— When young, and a parent begins: "this is not good"….invariably proves to be just that.

—— There are even times when the response: "I don't understand" may be truthful.

—— If you thought of all the illness it's possible to contract, just leaving your bedroom would elicit anxiety.

—— Most families are a mixture of personalities.

—— After the money's gone….it's back to reality.

—— A wise person once stated that in everything we do, we teach….and, only when absolutely necessary… we use words.

—— Angry, hurt people can, so often, also be uncompassionate, unforgiving people.

—— The challenge is to treat others even better, than they may be treating you.

—— Many times, it may be kinder to allow others to go through their challenge, than take it from them.

—— No matter how we feel, we can still choose to press past our feelings.

——— People who habitually hurt others are often acting out of their own pain.

——— Placing blame solves little.

——— Simply put: when we hurt others, we're hurting ourselves.

——— Think of how far you've come and gained.

——— Think of how much you've been helped by others.

——— At times, we may feel that we can't help the way we feel — but we can still try to control the way we feel.

——— Good decisions don't necessarily mean that they'll be easy to attain.

——— We've all been in a place, where we can use a little encouragement — and those around us "just don't get it".

——— Our final victory comes, only when we've managed to press on — to the end.

—— Too many spend more than they can afford.

—— Impulsive behavior is seldom productive behavior.

—— One of the worst sources from which to get our advice is our emotions.

—— Emotional stability has an endless list of advantages.

—— Important: we can mourn what we've lost or look forward to what we have left.

—— It can be really special when you find something that you didn't even realize you were seeking.

—— "Winging-it" is not the best way to handle your finances or run your life.

—— At any time — peace is priceless!

—— "Handling money" doesn't mean how quickly you're able to have it go through your fingers.

—— Justice from man is a hope. Justice from God is a Promise!

—— You're as old as you let others tell you you are.

—— Our past: a prison that many must escape, if freedom is to be possible.

—— Does food's flavor….just mean a combination of "salt and fat"?

—— "To wait" can often be one's best move.

—— There are those who find it easier to reach out to help — than to reach out for help.

—— It's not rare for many who are weak, to resent those who show strength.

—— There are times when we can understand life's happenings. There are many, many times when we don't.

—— It's remarkable, how many of life's trials, as well as life's solutions, share an astounding commonality.

—— Who are we to allow others little leeway for error?

—— If we're wise, we see — and learn from — the lessons of our lives.

—— The less we're willing to admit, the less we're willing to learn.

—— Housed in the heart of resentment is often envy.

—— A form of subtle cruelty is when we're simply not willing to "give the other person the satisfaction" of their position.

—— Looking back, we're better able to see and understand the evolution of our lives.

—— Our fears greatly deter our life's lessons to be learned.

—— Our fears greatly deter our good, from life's lessons learned.

—— It's not our job to always try to "make things right" for others.

—— Our plans may be intentions…but not absolutes.

———   As a society, we've now mastered ways to justify discrimination in much more deceptive ways.

———   As in a marriage, no government is either healthy or productive that lives only to get its own way.

———   Some people live a lifetime, not willing to admit that their parents were right.

———   If we had to understand everything before making a move, ours would be a very limited life.

———   There are times (even for those who give readily to others), when we just have to spoil ourselves.

———   Peace: derived and maintained from the world within us, not the world outside us.

———   Some of our greatest joys can also produce some of our greatest heartaches.

———   Did you ever wonder (and observe in awe) where man's instincts originate?

———   Our world still exists, represented by a relatively few "have(s)" and a multitude of "have not(s)".

—— A renewal of our Faith is seen when the "have(s)" offer a productive help and incentive to the "have not(s)".

—— Life would simply be so much more pleasant and enjoyable….if only those who could do…would do.

—— Courage: being willing to openly admit that we were on the wrong side of the issue.

—— Cowardness: never being able to admit — even after realizing it — that we were on the wrong side of an issue.

—— All those expensive, material possessions have no clout against a terminal, health diagnosis.

—— There are those who can keenly see our weaknesses, and if their motive is such, can/will exploit them.

—— Doing wrong (like doing right) can simply become a habit.

—— The other members of the animal world often adapt much more easily than humans do.

———   Some feelings, we simply can't explain.

———   Few parents want to discover, or admit, the weaknesses within one's offspring.

———   There really are a lot of things we could begin to understand, if we only took the time.

———   Ironically, there are times when the best thing to do is…nothing.

———   "Feeling out of place" is sometimes a good thing.

———   Many times, those with only minimal talent can have maximum enjoyment.

———   Making a profit is not necessarily the issue….to what extent and at what cost…is.

———   For some, their time becomes too precious a commodity...and as such...is unavailable.

———   Saying: "we've been married 36 years, and they've been the happiest 4 years of my life", says a lot.

—— Some of our battles take almost a lifetime to win —— or to concede.

—— Our pain is truly wasted, when it can never be used for good.

—— Some of the ones we love the most can be the most difficult to love.

—— At times, it may appear that our greatest love is toward those who deserve it the least.

—— Under stress, we're more prone to hurt others.

—— "Our heart's desire" is most easily changed with time and circumstance.

—— Being on the same "wave length" is good —— if that wave length is productive.

—— Our initial path in life can sometimes lead to quite different, and even better, paths.

—— Physical healing and emotional healing are not really separate entities.

—— Many of our prisons have been constructed in our own mind.

—— Feeling sorry for yourself is a dead-end street.

—— You may never be able to collect from people who feel that they don't owe you.

—— Emotional healing can take much longer than many types of physical healing.

—— We'll teach....whether that's our intended goal or not.

—— Too, too easily....we teach our children, our faults.

—— Marriage: one of life's greatest tests, in allowing us to maintain or to discard some of our greatest weaknesses.

—— To an undeniable extent, we are our "brother's keeper."

—— Not unfrequently, you may feel that the more you learn, the more questions you have.

—— For most, their trials are not staged in a courtroom.

—— Real, meaningful learning takes intent.

—— To temper our own "triggers," may be greatly helped by being aware of those of others.

—— "Diligence" is not an uncommonly-spoken word, but also an uncommonly-lived word.

—— If it's really something you want to do, you'll invariably find the time to do it.

—— There must always be a follow up to: "being inspired."

—— Rationalization covers a gamut of mental, emotional, physical, and social…failings.

—— "Trying to catch up" may exude a stressful tone, when starting a new day.

—— Whatever is done "begrudgingly" loses some essence of value.

—— Just "being available" can provide all the peace of mind that another needs.

—— Right answers only come to us when we quiet our mind and open our heart.

—— A wise person once said that we cannot use the same mind-set in solving our problems, that we used in creating them.

—— Two, heavy burdens we foolishly take on: being unable to accept forgiveness and being able to give it.

—— The fool finds no time to listen.

—— The fool finds no time to learn…or change.

—— Many good acts die in the "Cemetery of Thoughts."

—— True humility is a strength, not a weakness.

—— Too often, we see only what we want to see….and it becomes our loss.

— The breaking point of any ailment can be its longevity.

— Yes, there is such a mental exercise known as "creative thinking".

— What may cause us the greatest joy may be found in the giver, not the gift.

— "Complaining" usually intensifies our problems, rather than alleviating them.

— Problem: having more freedom than we're able to handle.

— Beware the words that find themselves in the midst of other words like: may/might, can/could, etc.

— Trying to change someone who doesn't share this goal: a definite loss for both involved.

— It may take a lifetime to learn one of life's greatest lessons: "what matters least."

— The "unexpected" isn't always bad!

—— If determined, some people will simply never change.

—— There really are those who invariably cling to hopeless causes.

—— Justice comes in many forms.

—— Giving away our wealth when one dies is commendable, but even more commendable, while one is still alive.

—— We all, at some point, will sin, however, not everyone will admit the offense. We all pay.

—— A peaceful Soul can't be bought. (Our most precious possessions can't be bought).

—— There are things that we should be afraid of.

—— Inactivity is a culprit in maintaining a healthy life.

—— Radiating health in all 3 realms: mentally, physically, and emotionally — is ultimate health.

—— For some, watching the evening news can become soothing to their own problematic woes.

—— At times, our best lessons are delivered in silence.

—— So many clueless people feel driven to volunteer in clueless endeavors.

—— Resistance can either help a situation or make it far worse.

—— Where my attention goes, my energy flows.

—— Having a path to stillness can be one of the greatest gifts in life.

—— Serious: losing the ability to relax.

—— My experiences are determined by my choices.

—— My words provide an avenue for my thoughts.

—— Holding on to resentment creates ongoing stress.

—— I am the keeper of my thoughts.

——— A peaceful mind is more receptive to possible solutions.

——— A thankful attitude changes our life's outlook for the good.

——— Many continue to believe that love is the most powerful force in the world.

——— Love helps us see the highest and best in others.

——— Most of the answers that we search for lie within us.

——— The power of our words can never be ignored.

——— Letting go of fear and limiting beliefs offer life a fresh start.

——— When we truly and seriously study the many forms of creation, we see a spectacular, underlying order.

——— Divine order is not found only in nature.

——— We gain nothing profitable, when we dwell on pessimism, lack, fear or doubt.

—— My choices and actions reflect the value that I place on life.

—— We are, and we become, what we believe.

—— To live in harmony with oneself becomes the best place to start.

—— Every once in a while, we should ask ourselves; "Who am I"? "What is my purpose"?

—— We actually place many of our restrictions on ourselves.

—— Some see themselves as one cell in the body of the Universe.

—— It has been written that when I am one with All That Is, "I am more of who I am".

—— When we renew our mind, we transform our life.

—— An inner transformation invariably prompts an outer one as well.

—— True wealth is not measured in monetary terms.

—— So often, life causes us to re-evaluate what has real meaning in our lives.

—— A great way to usher in a more healthy, happy life is to let go of worries, fears, and frustrations.

—— Beware: how habitual stress and anxiety destroy both mind and body.

—— Age can re-adjust our philosophy of life.

—— The human barriers we create result in the personal strife we live.

—— Every so many years, we should stop and ask ourselves: "what do I believe"? "What is important to me"?

—— One of the best ways to miss the present is to be engrossed or consumed about the future.

—— The mind of some people is like their belongings: "a cluster."

—— Talent is not always obvious; a lack of talent in a specific area usually is.

—— At times, even "seeing" isn't believing.

—— It's not usually a good idea to put things off:
forgiveness may be near the top of the list.

—— Sadly, too many people underestimate themselves
and minimize their capabilities.

—— It's unbelievable how many people are willing to
take unbelievable risks.

—— Some medicines have astounding results, only
because some people believe they will.

—— Wisdom is knowing what must be accepted and
what need not be.

—— Never good: trying to hold on to what has passed,
when it no longer serves a purpose.

—— "Worry" is always a bad investment.

—— Living without purpose…is not living.

—— In actuality, my thoughts, words, and intentions are
like a magnet.

——   Regret: putting off, and now it's too late, to extend the word or act to make things better.

——   At times, just a simple shift in our thinking can make all the difference.

——   Like laughter, joy is a state of mind and is contagious.

——   To mentally strengthen ourselves, we have to believe that we are capable, unique, and deserving.

——   Spring brings new birth; it brings a renewed sense of promise and potential.

——   Powerful and positive affirmative words and thoughts have been proven to promote life-sustaining health.

——   Faith and love — on a daily basis — work miracles!

——   Serenity is cultivated in silence.

——   Respect and cooperation foster understanding.

—— We are free, when we can let go of our feelings of unworthiness, shame, and guilt.

—— For most, showing compassion warms their hearts.

—— A key to living is knowing when to take action and when to take none.

—— True forgiveness is virtually an act of love.

—— Generally, the more we assume total control, the more frustrated we become.

—— Winning: moving through life's trials with assurance.

—— Words in many ways, can uncover differences.

—— Want to see a miracle? Watch the sprouts of new life pushing from beneath the winter's snow.

—— To quiet one's mind and heart can be one of the most difficult things for many to do.

—— Warning: when you're unable to be comfortable in the silence.

—— Sometimes, our answer is found just by shifting our perspective.

—— A guaranteed way to be miserable and alone: be gossipy, critical, or unkind, as a lifestyle.

—— Prayer is a gift; its root is love.

—— A day is truly wasted, if during it, we refuse to listen or to learn.

—— When we hold to our Faith, hope replaces doubt.

—— Circumstances have the power to distress us….if we let them.

—— Say good-bye to any emptiness from the past.

—— Very often, the most needed control we need is self-control.

—— Say: "what I do makes a difference"…because it does.

—— We all are given blessings; yet more than a few are overlooked.

—— Few could disagree that, at times, the world can be a sad and a scary place.

—— Self-imposed stress involves making our lives more impressive than they have to be.

—— Our appreciation of some of life's most special moments are lost, when we don't (or can't) slow down.

—— It's really a feat, in keeping our attention where it really belongs.

—— As humans, it's ludicrous to think (or believe) that we'll always get to do things our way.

—— Recipe for trouble: always jumping to our own, anxious conclusions.

—— How quickly our self-incrimination flees, when we choose to lighten up and laugh at ourselves.

—— Some prayers can be wordless.

—— Just being present can be a form of comfort.

—— For some, it takes a lifetime to discover what really matters.

—— At times, just learning how to persevere is a gift and talent.

—— Oh, so often, the answers to prayers are not what we expect.

—— The blessing and beauty of sleep is best discovered when it eludes us.

—— Re-hashing the past and fearing the future are among the two strongest ingredients for missing the present.

—— When we choose resentment, envy, or isolation… we choose wrong.

—— Childhood has lessons for adulthood.

—— "Trivial" is open to both opinion and translation.

—— Quite often, the physically strongest, most attractive and wealthiest….are not the happiest.

—— It's so easy to cause pain and disagreement, yet, so much harder to heal.

—— Some things never seem to grow old.

—— There are those who simply cannot look past themselves or their importance.

—— Generosity can be an attribute, but not when its motive can be questionable.

—— To be in a hurry is sometimes essential; as a lifestyle, it's usually not recommended.

—— Impatience is often the precursor to disaster.

—— "Encouragement" can be a positive or negative quality, depending on its motive.

—— Some things, we wish we didn't remember.

—— "To persevere" can be a form of noble behavior, or meager existence.

—— There are people who finally rest, not by permission, but only on command.

—— Sadly, some adopt healthier life styles when it's actually too late.

—— Hurtful and angry words, unfortunately, have a history of longevity.

—— Too many people have the characteristic of convenient forgetting.

—— We don't always want to see the "whole picture."

—— Many have the philosophy to prepare for the worst, yet to hope for the best.

—— Forgiveness: involves seeking it; granting it; and receiving it.

—— Lifelong friends are priceless!

—— At times, we see the blessing in having our own plans blocked.

—— Bottom line: what we do, matters.

—— Being overwhelmed with stress takes a negative toll on mind and body.

—— Many believe in the truth of the saying: "Peace begins with me."

—— Be good to those you love, while you're all still alive.

—— It can be very hard to both admit, and get rid of, our selfish ego.

—— To some degree, suffering is just part of living.

—— Oh, the love that our animals bring into our lives!

—— "Renewal" — another of life's gifts and possibilities.

—— "To give thanks" is medicine for the Soul.

—— It takes courage to reach out to those we've disappointed or hurt.

—— There are still doctors who are a blessing to those they treat.

—— There are also doctors whose demeanor is liken to certain "Wal-Mart" cashiers.

—— There are moments in our lives that cause us to carry lasting memories.

—— Even the small victories in our lives can lead to real transformations.

—— Admit it: our ways are not always the best.

—— We sometimes have to learn compassion for ourselves.

—— It's important to have the patience to live one day at a time.

—— The way we get up in the morning, more often than not, sets the tone for our day.

—— Life's trials and testing can actually add to our stability and increase our strength.

—— Beware: when someone has a suggestion or offer that just sounds too good.

—— Our healing can take place when we refuse to be a slave to the perception of others.

—— When our relationships know boundaries, we can avoid unnecessary stress.

—— We become truly happy, when we increase our self-awareness and begin to live our worth!

—— Always look for the good in life, even when it appears to be hidden.

—— I choose to let go of depression.

—— My Faith gives me confidence, courage, and clarity.

—— We can't solve our problems, when using the same thinking we used in creating them.

—— The place where my problems are solved lies deep within me — where wisdom lives.

—— By shifting my attention, new ideas take hold — also, where wisdom lives.

—— Our struggles begin to cease, when we shift our attention from a busy mind to a peaceful heart.

—— A change in attitude CAN make a difference between failure and success.

—— To reach our goals means pursuing them with perseverance and optimism.

—— "As we serve others," all of our lives can be enriched.

—— For some, peace is a stranger.

—— Emotions have the advantage that they're able to shift and change…for the better.

—— Fear makes us weak. It cripples us.

—— Nature teaches the needed cycles of life: clearing away the old; a period of rest; then new growth.

—— Too often, what we're afraid to expect — is what we actually get.

—— In many cases, it's not a question of transforming our image or outer appearance.

——— When we don't change our mindset, we don't change our life.

——— Every thought is a seed; the nature of our thoughts produces our harvest.

——— The way I view others affects and determines my interactions with them.

——— When our thoughts aren't at peace, our lives can't be at peace.

——— When we hold defensiveness or blame, healing and peace find no room.

——— There are people of all creeds who believe that man is a spiritual being, having a human appearance.

——— To be truly enjoyable, life must be filled with ongoing hope and great expectations.

——— When we argue against our inner voice of wisdom…we always lose.

——— The value of being connected with others can never be ignored or down-played.

—— Goals (great and small) can be accomplished when we work with others.

—— Want to see another miracle? — The way in which my body holds an innate ability to heal and restore.

—— Most people (at some point in time) would have done better, if they had listened, and not talked.

—— Our lives have seasons.

—— Our lives reflect our guiding principles: fear/worry or faith/trust.

—— When I try to control what others do, it only leads to my own frustration.

—— Setting someone else free to live their own life, I set myself free.

—— Love needs no words.

—— The breath of all living things is a miracle.

—— The Law of Increase is based on the principle that what I focus on, multiplies.

—— We grow, when we open our heart to learn.

—— Our lives are a reflection of our consciousness.

—— A shift in my consciousness can be changed, by examining my beliefs.

—— Our words carry power!

—— It's still much easier to live with the truth, than it is to live with a lie.

—— No one lives life without experiencing loss and challenges.

—— Life can be quiet torment, in repeating the lessons we continue to fail.

—— When all wealth is represented in material terms, it is unstable, at best.

—— How lenient we can be with those we like. How severe we can act toward those we don't.

—— People who are very spoiled have the same effect as food that is.

—— There can be many definitions of prosperity.

—— Love remains the greatest harmonizing force in the world.

—— To truly succeed, there must be a personal release of inadequacy and doubt.

—— My thankfulness and my peace of mind is my choice.

—— Admitting our weaknesses makes us stronger.

—— My state of mind affects everyone and everything in my life.

—— Bottom Line: we each have to assume responsibility for our own state of happiness.

—— We show our appreciation, by how we care for both people and things in our life.

—— When left to wander, our mind will often gravitate toward problems and unhappiness.

—— Defending a personal point of view can be both challenging and frustrating.

—— The power of our words can be either our solace or our downfall.

—— Share the wealth....and you'll always have something to share.

—— Many believe that all our prayers are answered.... just not all the way we want them to be.

—— We can easily squander our precious resources by abuse, neglect, and carelessness.

—— There are those who can only see the dark side of every situation.

—— Our well-being and happiness depend mainly on ourselves.

—— Music and dance can help release our doubts, worry, fear, and anxiety.

—— We each have "our own song" and "our own dance" to contribute to the world.

—— To be alive, enthusiastic and grateful is to have learned and applied the lessons of living.

—— I am always responsible for my own decisions.

—— Some days, it seems as if our patience is tested repeatedly.

—— Can you believe some of the advice that's offered? And accepted?

—— Technology, like computers, is amazing. In their abuse, and not their benefit, lies the problem.

—— There comes a time in virtually every life to release the need to know, life's every outcome.

—— Life is activity, movement, and growth.

—— Never be stingy with your gratitude.

—— Growth: when we open our mind and heart to new understanding.

—— The more clearly I understand myself, the better I'm able to understand the desires and needs of others.

——— Faith assures me of something more than my eyes can see or my mind can conceive.

——— We sometimes forget that we also need to be gentle with ourselves.

——— The body has a significant and miraculous power to heal itself.

——— A significant premise (and proof) is in knowing that our thoughts produce in like manner.

——— Mistakes may not prove beneficial, and they are often difficult to admit or justify.

——— Change your thoughts…change your life!

——— Ignorance can survive several generations.

——— Our creativity allows us to bring something into existence through our thoughts or behaviors.

——— Our expectations are powerful in shaping our experiences.

—— One of the best anecdotes for judgement is compassion.

—— The right practice can make real progress.

—— At times, when we look too closely at a problem, we can lose perspective.

—— Wisdom is knowing and accepting what is within my control and what isn't.

—— Much of our stress comes from self-imposed timelines.

—— Most people want to feel as if they belong.

—— The healthiest stance one can affirm, when faced with a challenge is: "I am able."

—— There are some people who are usually quite stingy, when it comes to encouragement.

—— Many have believed in the power of prayer — to renew, reinvigorate, and heal their loved ones.

—— Being peaceful lends itself to healing; being anxious lends itself to illness.

—— Most people find pleasure in the traditions they hold dear.

—— When I hold strongly to fear, anxiety, or anger, I create a negative outcome.

—— Life has a way of giving us what we strongly anticipate.

—— Routinely putting aside time for reflection appears to be a good, psychological principle.

—— In general, sleep can be quite healing.

—— When sleep eludes us, it tends to aggravate most ongoing maladies.

—— My thoughts greatly affect my physical and psychological health.

—— Actually, if desired, our destructive thoughts and habits can be changed.

—— Some people can only feel satisfied, when possessing a great number of material possessions.

—— To know peace can be an infrequent visitor.

—— Good friends often give the comfort that helps us through our challenges.

—— Our minds often want to automatically judge, analyze, and avoid any sudden happening.

—— My health and well-being are actually more determined by my "inner conditions," not outer conditions.

—— The best way to remain stagnant in our viewpoint is to have no room for others, as we solely clutch our own ideas.

—— Fear is often the first step toward defeat.

—— Fear is often the reason for immobility.

—— Flash: we can't rush results that have to unfold in their own time.

—— True patience is a silent energy that has the power to restore and strengthen.

—— Positive self-talk supports an intention to maintain our overall health.

—— For some, joy is only a slight, brief occurrence.... and it often shows.

—— The words "it's over" can have two, very different meanings.

—— Success is learning from my mistakes, picking myself up, and beginning again.

—— At times, we let our to-do list manage us, rather than the other way around.

—— Each event in life gives us the chance to heal and grow emotionally.

—— Sometimes we may feel as though we are our own worst enemy.

—— I create my life according to my beliefs....at each stage of my life.

—— Life's transformation can be gradual, yet dramatic.

—— We become powerless, when we allow others to determine how we should live.

—— When I open myself to receive it, inspiration comes to me through many channels.

—— Knowing the blessing of encouragement, look for opportunities to inspire others.

—— Achieving harmony takes practice.

—— Each day allows opportunities to learn and to grow.

—— Impulsive actions always demand a price to be paid.

—— Life is meant to be lived fully and intentionally.

—— The simplest act of kindness from one person to another can trigger a success of good deeds.

—— In times of need, a friend may be there.

—— I release everything that doesn't support my growth and well-being.

—— Let go and learn to enjoy.

—— Don't try to be someone else — just be yourself.

—— Calm down and cheer up.

—— We can easily become what we affirm and what we fear.

—— Our prayers are not always answered on our time-tables.

—— Unless relinquished, no one can take our Faith.

—— Unless relinquished, no one can take our Trust.

—— We have to unceasingly refuse to be used.

—— We have to unceasingly refuse to be intimidated.

—— We have to unceasingly refuse to be rejected.

——— Sadly, when returning, many of our Veterans are not equipped to join society's ongoing workplace.

——— Unfortunately, our returning Veterans do not find the emotional support to cope with society's demands.

——— There's wisdom in knowing when to continue and when to give in.

——— There's wisdom in knowing when to speak and when to be silent.

——— The seeming "impossible" sometimes just takes a little longer.

——— Potential gives birth to belief.

——— Faith is knowing that God Will.

——— Even true forgiveness can sometimes be accomplished in stages.

——— "Intended," in the realm of action is weak.

—— "Winging it" is not the best way to raise your children.

—— When we hold on to our Faith, hope replaces fear.

—— Some animals could teach humans about child rearing.

—— Some are never on "the same page".

—— Some people never seem to grow old.

—— Giving advice is never on a break.

—— Giving advice is never at a loss.

—— It's often easier to give advice, than to take it.

—— There are some who will never admit to being wrong.

—— Many wish to have more time, when nearing the end of one's life.

—— We often give little credit to those we dislike.

——— Oh, the excuses we make toward those we really like.

——— Oh, the faults we find in those we seem to dislike.

——— Many days are simply uneventful.

——— The best way to miss the present is to continue to be pre-occupied with the past.

——— It could be very productive to periodically stop and ask ourselves: "why do I believe what I do"?

——— At many times, "Not seeing is still believing."

——— Bad: making worry a way of life.

——— Investing an enormous amount of money to no avail — is not cost effective.

——— "Almost" is often a coward's rhetoric.

——— "Sometime" can be a frustrating chant.

—— Giving what you need can often be the greatest blessing.

—— Oh, how we hoard that which we never use.

—— How overwhelmingly debilitating "fear" can become.

—— Justice comes in many forms. Justice from man is a hope. Justice from God is a promise!

—— Being alone can be an advantage or a curse.

—— Everything "in happy medium" appears to be the healthiest way to go.

—— Only a fool always chases the path of self-reliance.

—— Some people just can't admit when they're wrong.

—— If you want to stay unhappy — don't forgive.

—— Our secrets are often fodder for our downfall.

—— Serious: losing the ability or desire to listen to others.

—— Too many are running too fast….and accomplishing too little.

—— Knowing one's faults is not the problem…. admitting them is the ongoing task.

—— Sometimes, we just have to do nothing.

—— Trying too hard is as damaging as trying too little.

—— Choosing "the one we listen to" is often a frustrating choice.

—— Limited travel often means a limited perspective.

—— It's so much easier to see the faults in others…than in ourselves.

—— Few people welcome criticism….however, few people can resist giving it.

—— There still remains somewhat of a stigma when "doctoring" involves the psychological, and not the physical domain.

—— So many go through life needing the praises of others to determine their own self-worth.

—— Unfortunately, we may gain wisdom, when we have limited time to employ it.

—— Most people are actually good people.

—— To a great extent, our ideas in adulthood have been formulated in our youth.

—— Avoidance is sometimes impossible.

—— Good ideas are sometimes "bad ideas — rethought".

—— Still, few people are truly "color blind."

—— Unfortunately, ignorance is easily passed on.

—— A truly educated person can possess little or no academic standing.

—— "Listening" has become a lost art, in many circles.

—— Oh, to re-capture the magic of youth!

—— The saddest of thoughts in old age come under the category of regrets.

—— Ironically, often, the more we give away, the more we seem to get.

—— Much of life means manual, repetitive tasks.

—— Tax time can be stress time.

—— Keep it simple…keep it honest.

—— Woe to the person who is easily swayed or weak in one's personal convictions.

—— Going to the doctor or dentist still creates a nervousness in many adults.

—— Most things aren't as bad as feared.

—— "Putting things off" is just a subtle form of frustration.

—— "Repeating" can become really frustrating to the audience involved.

—— Few people always say what they're thinking.

—— Youth just has to be youth….in order to get smarter.

—— No one sounds smart all the time.

—— No one said getting older is without its disadvantages.

—— At times, we're glad we stopped and didn't say what we almost did.

—— Sometimes, we're harder on ourselves than anyone else could ever be.

—— Talent doesn't always run in families.

—— Not all parents are encouraging.

——— There are those who define life as a constant battle.

——— Ego is interesting. For some, it's defined in the home one owns, the car one drives, or the clothes one wears.

——— For most, ego is modified with age.

——— Many people, at some point, view the progress they've made, just by living.

——— Oh, how our likes and dislikes change as we age!

——— Oh, how our wants and needs change as we age!

——— How fast time goes!

——— NEVER go through life sad and scared.

——— We are meant to live life with Faith and Joy.

——— Most people believe the "workings of Karma" to some extent.

—— At your class reunions, you still probably think you look the best.

—— There are still so many things we just can't control.

—— There's always a "trade-off" with most of our important choices.

—— Many people are "joiners" at some point in their lives.

—— Oh, how stubborn we can be!

—— Many children grow up at the rate of their parents.

—— Want a heated discussion? — Discuss religion or politics.

—— We often defend our life's choices.

—— Some winters seem never-ending.

—— Cruelty to animals is near unforgivable.

——— Ever try to cut your own hair? Ever think the hair would never grow back?

——— No one likes a complainer.

——— There are those who are quick to give advice to almost everyone.

——— No brutality from anyone or any group should go unpunished.

——— Our children are watching.

——— Some hope that their reputation will not be based on the car they drive. Some really don't care.

——— There are definite struggles that are part of the aging process.

——— Are you starting to see your parents in you?

——— Oh, how boisterous we can become at our children's athletic competitions.

——— How quickly we can defend those we love.

—— Simply put: there are those who are "cheap."

—— Somehow, we'll find the money for something we really want.

—— To survive is normally one of man's greatest desires.

—— We can be known as different people to different individuals.

—— To lack purpose is to lack a lust for living.

—— You've got to have a goal!

—— Feeling hopeless is serious and dangerous.

—— Some people find joy in the smallest of things.

—— We may feel badly about the background of our parents....but it was theirs.

—— "To escape" has many meanings to many people.

——— Woe to some "coach's children" who have no interest in athletics.

——— Not everyone is meant to be a teacher.

——— Not everyone was meant to be a doctor.

——— There are some who simply aren't nice people.

——— There are some really nice people.

——— Unfortunately, too many people still try to live their children's lives.

——— So many commercials to so many programs!

——— Knowing is often not synonymous with doing.

——— We were meant to live only our own life.

——— Most "easily gotten" money is easily lost.

——— No one has all the answers, but some have lived and know a few of them.

—— Jealousy takes a human toll.

—— Sometimes, just boasting "survival" is as good as it gets.

—— Choosing Christmas gifts for one's grandchildren becomes more difficult with age.

—— Choosing to give money to our grandchildren at Christmas is often the best choice — for all.

—— With age, it's far too easy to become isolated from family and friends.

—— Some areas offer little social opportunities for seniors.

—— Having will-power can never be down-played.

—— Some physicians simply have no (or little) bedside manner.

—— Generally speaking, "moderation" is often the best technique.

——— Most people are thoroughly aware of their weaknesses — and need no reminders.

——— There are those who simply have an "infectious laugh."

——— Beware! Some have an answer for everything.

——— God is watching! Some believe we do not answer for our life's deeds — some are wrong.

——— There are those who never seem to find their calling, in vocational terms.

——— No one likes a whiner.

——— No one likes a loud-mouth.

——— It's easy to have Faith, when everything is going well.

——— To succeed, our Faith must be greater than our fear.

——— "Making another's day," may just involve a quick phone call.

—— We are what we believe!

—— We can help, but not do what someone else is doing.

—— Oh, when sleep evades you!

—— There are those who look to find fault.

—— To escape is normally a time-dictated luxury.

—— God's law, unlike man's law is perfect and eternal.

—— Many wealthy people find it difficult to relate to the very poor.

—— Many wait a little too long to spoil themselves, after they've had the means to do so.

—— Sometimes, it just means that you're willing to try.

—— Some of our acts provide no re-takes.

—— There really are those who don't know what to wear to certain functions.

—— Making fun of others is often a cover-up for one's own insecurities.

—— Most people are dissatisfied with some aspect of their looks.

—— Not everyone agrees with many of the government's edicts.

—— So much is taken for granted.

—— Not everyone should have a pet.

—— There are those who just "talk a good tale."

—— Few get paid what they think they're worth.

—— Some get paid more than their actual worth.

—— Dreams are good. Fulfillment is better.

—— There are some people who take the opposite position; they just crave opposition.

—— "Peace" can be a fleeting or an ongoing experience.

—— Not everyone who teaches...should...or can.

—— Sometimes, just being "willing" is all that's needed.

—— It may begin as a dream; hopefully, that's not where it ends.

—— People often find they could do much more than they thought they could.

—— You can't buy Peace of Mind.

—— Growing older is no guarantee to getting smarter.

—— New technology is mind-boggling to many seniors.

—— Some days you really wish you could stay in bed.

—— If you think you've learned it all....it's very likely you have much to learn.

—— It's good to be confident, but perhaps not overly confident.

—— A parent's reward: seeing one's children as "truly good people."

—— Sometimes, we just accidentally do what's right.

—— There's such a thing as: "just trying too hard."

—— Everyone seems to have an opinion.

—— Not everyone has a good opinion.

—— "Politicians" and "promises" seem to go hand-in-hand.

—— Cruelty is found in an array of forms.

—— Ignorance is found in many forms.

—— A "mind set" can be an unfortunate attribute.

—— "Just being oneself" may not always be a commendable attribute.

—— Sometimes, we just want — and have — to be alone.

—— Many of the best things in life, we must acquire on our own.

—— Guilt can take a lifetime to resolve. To be truly at peace or happy, guilt must be resolved.

—— No one's perfect. Some just think they are.

—— Sometimes, the best thing to do is…nothing.

—— There's always something you can get excited about.

—— House cleaning can seem like an endless job.

—— A more peaceful demeanor can begin with an intentional deep breath.

—— Everyone needs a break from time to time.

—— Beware: when you can't stand silence for an extended period of time.

—— No one's perfect. Some just pretend to be.

——— To be able to really relax is really a gift.

——— Beware the philosophy: "one of these days…."

——— Be always aware of just how fast the time of your life is going.

——— Trying something different can be good for the Soul.

——— Anticipate the positive — don't always fear the negative.

——— Faith, like fear, can become a habit….but Faith is a good habit.

——— "We are what we think."

——— Without effort, we can still make ourselves tired.

——— There are those who live just "to rock the boat."

——— There are those who find little, or no, joy in anything.

—— Changing opinions isn't always a bad thing.

—— "Wasting time" actually is a punishable offense.

—— A fixed income is also known as "social security."

—— Few people are totally proud of their background.

—— Hopefully, our mistakes are leading us to a greater good.

—— "Growing old," is a given.

—— Most people find some fault with the looks they've inherited.

—— Not everyone decides to take a walk "on the wild side."

—— Many live their lives on the conservative side.

—— Peace of Mind is one of the greatest blessings man can attain.

—— Some pay more attention to their neighbor's affairs, than their own.

—— A misery in life is living next door to a spiteful neighbor.

—— Some political battles have gone on for decades — to no avail.

—— "Money" is often a classic, marital battleground.

—— Some battle weight problems all their lives.

—— The extremes in life should normally be avoided.

—— At times, our initial disappointments have turned out to be our blessings.

—— It's what we accumulate that can prove to be a blessing or a downfall.

—— No one wants to be criticized.

—— There are those who always find an opening to criticize others.

—— There are those who speak as if their audience is always hard of hearing.

—— Some do not appear as candidates for parenthood.

—— Man's toys vary with man's age.

—— There are children who never seem to grow up.

—— There are adults who have an excuse for everything that happens.

—— People vary in the talents they've been given.

—— There are those with extended hands — not just to take, but to give.

—— To truly understand, sometimes takes a lifetime.

—— We may not always do our best — we can always try.

—— Sometimes, it's okay to be lazy. Sometimes.

—— Most days and people aren't that exciting.

—— It can be a blessing or a curse, in knowing when our life will end.

—— Not everyone welcomes "surprises."

—— Announcement: we don't always get what we want!

—— Depressing words: "too late."

—— There are people who give, looking for nothing in return.

—— Summers can sometimes seem, too short.

—— There are those who just can't take a compliment.

—— At times, many are working at jobs that they really dislike.

—— Lying to God is futile.

—— Usually, time moves faster than we want.

—— Chances are, there will always be someone who doesn't like you.

—— Chances are, there will always be someone whom you don't like.

—— Time is seldom a guarantee for life.

—— At times, there's no one to hear our joy.

—— Often, it seems like there's no one listening.

—— Complaints can often be useless and disregarded.

—— Over time, more plots to get your money become prevalent.

—— Renting, instead of buying a home, appears to have become more popular.

—— Depending on the renters, life can become an on-going nightmare to owners.

—— Not everyone is interested in sports. Difficult to fathom, for those who are.

—— "Universal Healthcare" has been on the docket for generations now.

—— Politics can be a disheartening topic.

—— Any two people will probably not always agree.

—— Some people don't know how to calmly disagree.

—— There are those who will never make peace.

—— There are those who should not have married —
each other.

—— There's always hope — if that's the goal.

—— Who would have thought to see the original
telephone become so outdated?

—— When "Ultimate Justice" is totally believed, no
harm or injustice has power over us.

—— Don't pass judgement — especially if you have not
been physically involved.

—— The Human Spirit is miraculous.

—— Did you ever wonder, if possible, what your pet would say?

—— "God speaks in silences."

—— Never judge, without any type of proof — even better, never judge.

—— Man wasn't meant to be alone.

—— There are some people who you may never, really understand.

—— Just do your best! You'll never please everyone, anyway.

—— Don't waste time on re-living past mistakes.

—— Life requires us to be serious at times, but not serious all the time.

—— Not everyone grows up and matures.

—— Money was meant to be spent — not only saved and hoarded.

—— Not everyone is meant to have a pet.

—— Time lost is one of man's greatest losses.

—— Man's "phones" have often replaced man's need for a mutual, verbal discourse.

—— Money will never replace "time lost."

—— Some children are physical representations of one or both of their parents.

—— We often avoid what we feel inept at facing.

—— Not everyone has to always agree.

—— Those who politically disagree should also be seen to vote.

—— Too many are driven by emotional drives, not educated concepts.

—— Too many spend energies complaining, but not doing.

——— Being educated on an issue does not require evidence of a college degree.

——— No college diploma guarantees "common sense."

——— No college diploma guarantees a kind heart.

——— Taking time out for oneself isn't spoiling oneself — it's a necessity.

——— Beware the extremes in life.

——— No one is right all the time!

——— Take heart: you're probably not wrong all the time. Probably not.

——— Life is a "give and take" process. Neither extreme is a healthy one, however.

——— Using common sense can be a slippery slope for some.

——— Always trying to prove yourself "right," can be an exhaustive ordeal.

—— Some suffer a feeling of devastation, if losing an argument.

—— There are many definitions to the term "winner."

—— There are many definitions to the term "loser."

—— Let go of the criticism in your life.

—— Our age can often be identified by the music we know, and if such, the words we still remember.

—— Beware self-diagnosis, using medical books.

—— Physical and mental diagnoses should be left to the medical practitioners.

—— We don't lie to God.

—— Sometimes animals are much wiser than their owners.

—— Without humor, life would be morose.

—— Stupid and irresponsible is no way to travel through life.

—— Weight "gurus" are a big business in today's world.

—— Too many Americans are over-weight, or lose weight, then regain it again.

—— In life, generally speaking, extremes are unhealthy.

—— Some people find problems, wherever they move.

—— Being critical seems to come naturally to some people.

—— "Finding fault" seems to have been perfected by certain individuals.

—— The rewards of exercise are often best accomplished in moderation.

—— Many find fault with the looks and dress of others.

—— Some undertake extreme methods to change the looks they've inherited.

—— Without Peace, no earthly goods matter.

—— Man is comprised of both body and Spirit....each affect the other.

—— Man also requires moments of serenity.

—— Don't depend on others to define you.

—— Practicing gratitude even enhances our personal demeanor.

—— Today and every day, celebrate life.

—— Happiness: when we allow nothing to disturb our Soul's peace.

—— We can discover our own worth, in the process of serving others.

—— Our mistakes are to lead to our greater good.

—— We all need to be comforted, at times.

—— Obstacles in life are a given.

—— No one said that forgiving would always be easy.

—— Some people create their own obstacles in life.

—— "Patience" truly is a virtue.

—— In time, we can begin to discover the Order in the Universe.

—— "Freedom of choice" can prove to be a blessing or a curse.

—— A worthy goal: to help create harmony and peace.

—— A healthy attitude: see life as an environment of healthy possibilities.

—— We can even do small things with great love.

—— With little effort of discovery: there are numerous places where you can serve.

—— Have Faith! Not fear.

—— "Hearing and listening" are definitely not the same.

——— To be a worthy caregiver is not easy.

——— As a life-style, focus on the good, not the bad.

——— When we are centered in Faith, we expect the best.

——— There is such a thing as Divine Wisdom.

——— Our perspective is our destiny.

——— What we affirm becomes the guidelines of our life.

——— The "Good Life" — has a zest and enthusiasm.

——— Many live with the belief that we are Divinely protected.

——— It's crucial to also forgive oneself.

——— My thoughts are my life's blueprint.

——— We must make many unending difficult choices in life.

—— Patience is, indeed, a virtue.

—— Hopefully, as we grow older, we grow wiser.

—— We are given many opportunities to change our lives.

—— Some people seem to resist virtually everything that is presented.

—— Many find peace in the process of meditation and yoga.

—— At times, we must have to surrender to life.

—— Life reflects a balance when our mind, body, and spirit are in alignment.

—— At times, it's difficult to just be still, and listen.

—— Difficult, but necessary, is to release anything that no longer serves us.

—— We should open our mind and heart to ongoing, new perspectives.

—— I, alone, often decide what kind of day I'm going to have.

—— Through Faith, we can make a difference.

—— Let go of worry and doubt. Be free from fear.

—— Do you ever wonder how some drivers got their license?

—— Change: to be viewed as a fear or an opportunity.

—— The goal is not to live longer and get dumber.

—— Realizing our mistakes is just our first step.

—— Just because you can have children, should not be the needed or only requirement.

—— I stop telling God how big my problem is; instead, I start telling my problem….how big my God is!

—— I am comforted and reassured; whatever the situation, I can relax, let go, and let God.

——— Face life with Faith, Hope, Love, and Forgiveness.
Life is a test....these are some of its answers.